W9-AFZ-853

Volume 2 Topics 9-15

Authors

Randall I. Charles
Professor Emeritus
Department of Mathematics
San Jose State University
San Jose, California

Jennifer Bay-Williams
Professor of Mathematics Education
College of Education and Human
Development
University of Louisville
Louisville, Kentucky

Robert Q. Berry, III
Associate Professor of
Mathematics Education
Department of Curriculum,
Instruction and Special Education
University of Virginia
Charlottesville, Virginia

Janet H. Caldwell
Professor of Mathematics
Rowan University
Glassboro, New Jersey

Zachary Champagne
Assistant in Research
Florida Center for Research in Science,
Technology, Engineering, and
Mathematics (FCR-STEM)
Jacksonville, Florida

Juanita Copley
Professor Emerita, College of Education
University of Houston
Houston, Texas

Warren Crown
Professor Emeritus of Mathematics
Education
Graduate School of Education
Rutgers University
New Brunswick, New Jersey

Francis (Skip) Fennell
L. Stanley Bowlsbey Professor
of Education and Graduate and
Professional Studies
McDaniel College
Westminster, Maryland

Karen Karp
Professor of Mathematics Education
Department of Early Childhood and
Elementary Education
University of Louisville
Louisville, Kentucky

Stuart J. Murphy
Visual Learning Specialist
Boston, Massachusetts

Jane F. Schielack
Professor of Mathematics
Associate Dean for Assessment and
Pre K-12 Education, College of Science
Texas A&M University
College Station, Texas

Jennifer M. Suh
Associate Professor for
Mathematics Education
George Mason University
Fairfax, Virginia

Jonathan A. Wray
Mathematics Instructional Facilitator
Howard County Public Schools
Ellicott City, Maryland

SAVVAS
LEARNING COMPANY

SAVVAS
LEARNING COMPANY

ISBN-13: 978-0-328-88715-6
ISBN-10: 0-328-88715-3
11 2022

Digital Resources

You'll be using these digital resources throughout the year!

Go to SavvasRealize.com

 MP
Math Practices **Animations** to play anytime

 Glossary
Animated Glossary in English and Spanish

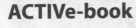 **Help**
Another Look Homework Video for extra help

ACTIVe-book
Student Edition online for showing your work

 Solve
Solve & Share problems plus math tools

 Tools
Math Tools to help you understand

 Games
Math Games to help you learn

 Learn
Visual Learning Animation Plus with animation, interaction, and math tools

 Assessment
Quick Check for each lesson

 eText
Student Edition online

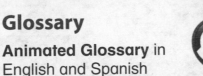 **SAVVAS realize** Everything you need for math anytime, anywhere

Contents

KEY

- Operations and Algebra
- Numbers and Computation
- Measurement and Data
- Geometry

Digital Resources at SavvasRealize.com

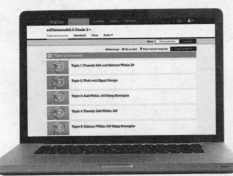

And remember your eText is available at SavvasRealize.com!

TOPICS

SavvasRealize.com

TOPIC 9
Numbers to 1,000

This shows how you can make 259 using place-value blocks.

Contents

TOPIC 10
Add Within 1,000 Using Models and Strategies

This shows how you can draw models and regroup to find 173 + 244.

SavvasRealize.com

Contents

F7

TOPIC 11
Subtract Within 1,000 Using Models and Strategies

This shows one way to count back to subtract on an open number line to find 580 − 232.

$$-2 \quad -30 \quad -200$$

348 350   380   580

Contents

This shows how to measure to the nearest inch. The eraser is about 2 inches long.

INCHES

halfway mark

TOPIC 12
Measuring Length

SavvasRealize.com

TOPIC 13
More Addition, Subtraction, and Length

This shows how you can represent whole numbers as lengths on a number line.

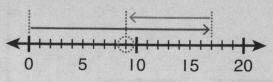

Amelia walks 17 blocks before dinner. She walks 8 blocks after dinner.

How many more blocks does she walk before dinner than after dinner?

Contents

TOPIC 14
Graphs and Data

This picture graph shows data and can be used to solve problems.

Favorite Ball Games	
Baseball	�% �%ç
Soccer	☎☎☎☎☎☎☎☎
Tennis	☎☎☎☎

Each ☎ = 1 student

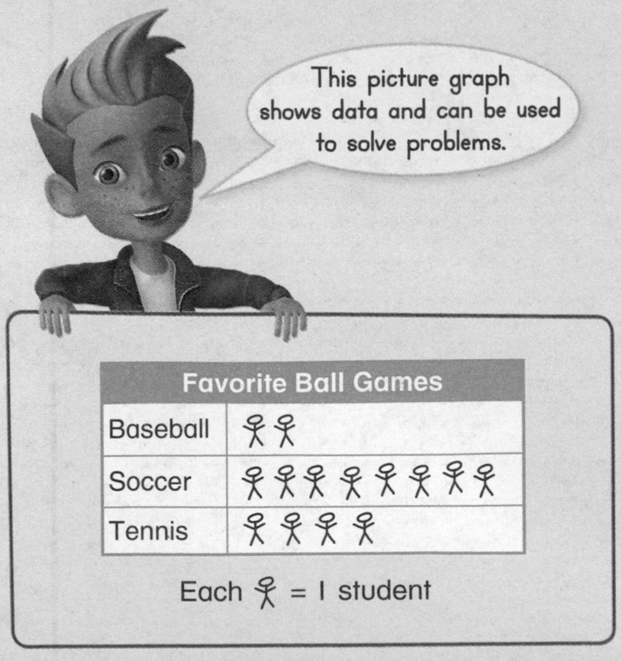

TOPIC 15
Shapes and Their Attributes

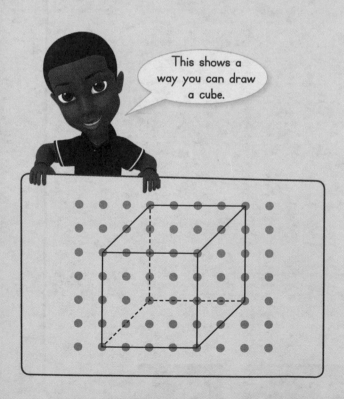

This shows a way you can draw a cube.

Contents

STEP UP to Grade 3

These lessons help prepare you for Grade 3.

Problem Solving Handbook

Problem Solving Handbook

Math Practices

1 Make sense of problems and persevere in solving them.

2 Reason abstractly and quantitatively.

3 Construct viable arguments and critique the reasoning of others.

4 Model with mathematics.

5 Use appropriate tools strategically.

6 Attend to precision.

7 Look for and make use of structure.

8 Look for and express regularity in repeated reasoning.

There are good Thinking Habits for each of these math practices.

1 Make sense of problems and persevere in solving them.

Good math thinkers know what the problem is about. They have a plan to solve it. They keep trying if they get stuck.

My plan is to use counters as trucks. I can act out the problem.

A store has some toy trucks.
Mike buys 2 of the trucks.
Now the store has 3 trucks.
How many trucks did the store have at the start?

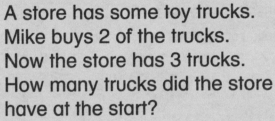

5 – 2 = 3
5 trucks

Thinking Habits

What do I need to find?

What do I know?

What's my plan for solving the problem?

What else can I try if I get stuck?

How can I check that my solution makes sense?

MP (2) **Reason abstractly and quantitatively.**

I completed a part-part-whole model. It shows how things in the problem are related.

Good math thinkers know how to think about words and numbers to solve problems.

Tony has 10 apples. 6 are red. The rest are green. How many apples are green?

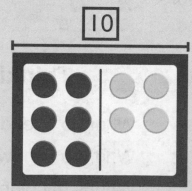

10

$10 - 6 = 4$

4 apples are green.

Thinking Habits

What do the numbers stand for?

How are the numbers in the problem related?

How can I show a word problem using pictures or numbers?

How can I use a word problem to show what an equation means?

Problem Solving Handbook

3 Construct viable arguments and critique the reasoning of others.

I can use place-value blocks to check Paula's thinking. My explanation is clear and complete.

Good math thinkers use math to explain why they are right. They talk about math that others do, too.

Paula added 34 + 5.
She says she had to regroup the ones.
Is she correct? Show how you know.

34 has 4 ones.
4 ones and 5 ones are 9 ones.
Paula is incorrect.
You do not need to regroup ones.

Tens	Ones

34 + 5 = 39

Thinking Habits

How can I use math to explain my work?

Am I using numbers and symbols correctly?

Is my explanation clear?

What questions can I ask to understand other people's thinking?

Are there mistakes in other people's thinking?

Can I improve other people's thinking?

4 Model with mathematics.

I can use ten-frames and counters to show the problem.

Good math thinkers use math they know to show and solve problems.

14 dogs are playing at a park.
9 dogs go home.
How many dogs are still at the park?

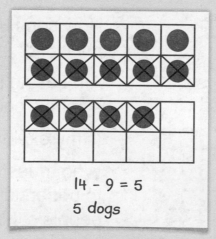

14 – 9 = 5
5 dogs

Thinking Habits

How can I use the math I know to help solve this problem?

Can I use a drawing, diagram, table, graph, or objects to show the problem?

Can I write an equation to show the problem?

F20

Problem Solving Handbook

MP

5 Use appropriate tools strategically.

Good math thinkers know how to pick the right tools to solve math problems.

I chose connecting cubes to solve the problem.

Kai and Maddie each pick 6 apples.
Then Maddie picks 1 more apple.
How many apples do they pick in all?

6 + 7 = 13

13 apples

Thinking Habits

Which tools can I use?

Is there a different tool I could use?

Am I using the tool correctly?

6 Attend to precision.

> Good math thinkers are careful about what they write and say, so their ideas about math are clear.

> I can use the definition of a cube to help me describe what it looks like.

Circle each cube below.

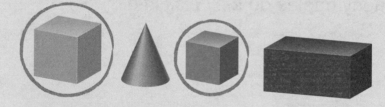

Describe what a cube looks like.

A cube has 6 flat surfaces.

Each flat surface is the same size.

A cube has 12 edges.

Thinking Habits

Am I using numbers, units, and symbols correctly?

Am I using the correct definitions?

Is my answer clear?

Problem Solving Handbook

7 Look for and make use of structure.

It is hard to add three numbers at once. I can add any two numbers first. I added 6 + 4 first to make the problem easier.

Good math thinkers look for patterns in math to help solve problems.

Jeff saw 6 brown frogs, 3 green frogs, and 4 spotted frogs.
How many frogs did Jeff see in all?

Show your work and explain your answer.

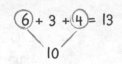

⑥ + 3 + ④ = 13

10

I made 10 then added 3 to make the problem easier.

Thinking Habits

Is there a pattern?

How can I describe the pattern?

Can I break the problem into simpler parts?

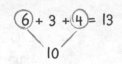

8 Look for and express regularity in repeated reasoning.

MP

I can compare the tens first. If the tens are the same, I can compare the ones.

Good math thinkers look for things that repeat in a problem. They use what they learn from one problem to help them solve other problems.

Compare each pair of numbers. Write <, >, or =. Tell how you will compare each pair of numbers.

57 (<) 75   49 (<) 52

36 (>) 34   61 (=) 61

Thinking Habits

Does something repeat in the problem?

How can the solution help me solve another problem?

Problem Solving Handbook

Problem Solving Guide

These questions can help you solve problems.

Make Sense of the Problem

Reason
- What do I need to find?
- What given information can I use?
- How are the quantities related?

Think About Similar Problems
- Have I solved problems like this before?

Persevere in Solving the Problem

Model with Math
- How can I use the math I know?
- How can I show the problem?
- Is there a pattern I can use?

Use Appropriate Tools
- What math tools could I use?
- How can I use those tools?

Check the Answer

Make Sense of the Answer
- Is my answer reasonable?

Check for Precision
- Did I check my work?
- Is my answer clear?
- Is my explanation clear?

Some Ways to Show Problems
- Draw a Picture
- Draw a Number Line
- Write an Equation

Some Math Tools
- Objects
- Rulers
- Technology
- Paper and Pencil

Problem Solving Recording Sheet

This sheet helps you organize your work.

Name **Mary**

Teaching Tool
1

Problem Solving Recording Sheet

Problem:
John bikes for 17 miles on Monday.
He bikes for 15 miles on Tuesday.
How many miles does John bike in all?

MAKE SENSE OF THE PROBLEM

Need to Find

I need to find how many miles John bikes in all.

Given

John bikes 17 miles on Monday and 15 miles on Tuesday.

PERSEVERE IN SOLVING THE PROBLEM

Some Ways to Represent Problems
☑ Draw a Picture
☐ Draw a Number Line
☑ Write an Equation

Some Math Tools
☐ Objects
☐ Rulers
☐ Technology
☑ Paper and Pencil

Solution and Answer

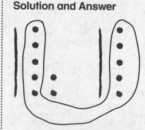

$17 + 15 = 32$

I made a 10.
John bikes 32 miles in all.

CHECK THE ANSWER

I checked my drawing of blocks.
They matched the problem and show 32 in all.

TT1

Numbers to 1,000

Essential Question: How can you count, read, and show numbers to 1,000?

Digital Resources

Solve Learn Glossary

Tools Assessment Help Games

Look at the model of a bird! How many pieces do you think it took to make it?

What else could you make with the same pieces?

Wow! Let's do this project and learn more.

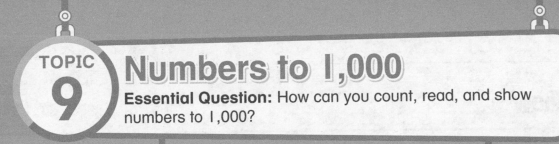

Math and Science Project: Breaking Apart and Putting Together

Find Out Collect sets of building blocks. Take turns and work together. Use the blocks to build a model. Then take that model apart and use the same blocks to build a different model.

Journal: Make a Book Show your models in a book. In your book, also:

• Tell how many pieces you used to build your models.

• Show how to use place-value blocks to model different names for the same number.

Name _____

Review What You Know

A-Z Vocabulary

1. Circle the coin with the **least value**. Put a square around the coin with the **greatest value**.

2. Circle the number that has 5 **ones** and 4 **tens**.

54

45

40

5

3. Tom is having breakfast. The minute hand on the clock shows **half past 7 o'clock**. Circle the time on the clock.

7:15 a.m.

7:30 a.m.

7:15 p.m.

7:30 p.m.

Counting Money

4. Circle coins that total 83¢.

Breaking Apart Numbers

5. Break apart each number into tens and ones.

23 = _____ + _____

47 = _____ + _____

96 = _____ + _____

Math Story

6. Howie has $13. A backpack costs $30. How much more money does Howie need to buy the backpack?

$_____

My Word Cards

Study the words on the front of the card.
Complete the activity on the back.

A-Z
Glossary

hundred

thousand

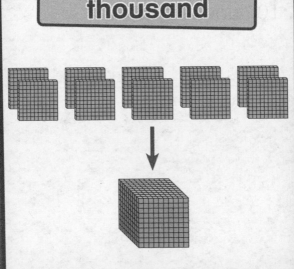

digits

43	815
2 digits	3 digits

place-value chart

Hundreds	Tens	Ones
3	4	8

expanded form

$$400 + 60 + 5$$

standard form

$$465$$

My Word Cards

Numbers are made up of
1 or more

_____.

10 hundreds make 1

_____.

10 tens make 1

_____.

_____

is a way to write a number
using only its digits.

_____

is a way to write a number
showing the place value of
each digit.

A _____

_____

matches each digit of a
number with its place.

My Word Cards

Study the words on the front of the card.
Complete the activity on the back.

---

word form

four hundred
sixty-five

---

compare

> < =

---

greater than (>)

$325 > 299$

---

less than (<)

$411 < 438$

---

equals (=)

$75 = 75$

---

increase

$224 \rightarrow 324 \rightarrow 424$

increase by 100

My Word Cards

325 is _____

_____ 299.

When you _____

numbers, you find out if a number is greater than, less than, or equal to another number.

_____

is a way to write a number using only words.

Numbers that

_____

become greater in value.

---

75 _____ 75.

---

411 is _____

_____ 438.

A-Z Glossary

My Word Cards

Study the words on the front of the card.
Complete the activity on the back.

decrease

424 → 324 → 224

decrease by 100

My Word Cards

Use what you know to complete the sentences.
Extend learning by writing your own sentence using each word.

Numbers that

____

become lesser in value.

Name _____

Another Look! You can show hundreds with models.

Circle the models to show 500.

500 equals ___5___ hundreds, 0 tens, and 0 ones.

Count by 100s to find 500.

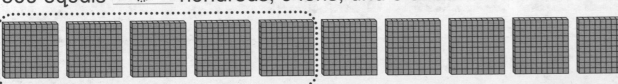

Remember that 10 ones = 1 ten , 10 tens = 1 hundred

and 10 hundreds = 1 thousand .

HOME ACTIVITY Ask your child to count by hundreds to solve the following problem. *Each box of paper clips has one hundred paper clips. Joe has 6 boxes of paper clips. How many paper clips does Joe have in all?*

Circle the models to show each number. Write the number of hundreds.

1. 200   How many hundreds? _____

2. 700   How many hundreds? _____

3. 900   How many hundreds? _____

4. 1,000   How many hundreds? _____

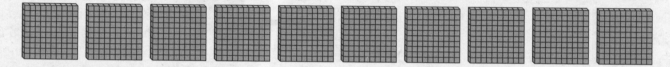

Solve each problem below.

5. Use tens blocks to build 100. Think about how many tens make 100. Draw a picture of your model.

6. Higher Order Thinking Patrick picked two numbers. The first number has 7 hundreds, 0 tens, and 0 ones. The second number has 2 fewer hundreds than the first number. Which two numbers did Patrick pick?

Patrick's numbers are _____

and _____.

7. ✅ Assessment Each bag has 100 pretzels. Count by hundreds to find the total. Which is the total number of pretzels in the bags?

Ⓐ 150   Ⓑ 400   Ⓒ 500   Ⓓ 550

Name _____

Another Look! Use models and your workmat to sort and count.

First, put the hundreds flats on your mat. Next, put the tens rods on your mat. Last, put the ones cubes on your mat.

Write the number of hundreds, tens, and ones.

HOME ACTIVITY Give your child 50 paper clips or other small, countable objects. Ask your child how many ones make 5 tens.

Hundreds	Tens	Ones
2	4	3

Write the numbers.
Use models and your workmat if needed.

1.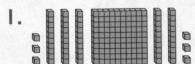

Hundreds	Tens	Ones

2.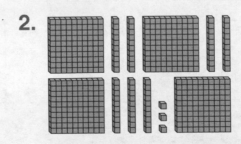

Hundreds	Tens	Ones

Solve each problem. Use models and your workmat if needed.

3. **Model** Write the number based on the model shown.

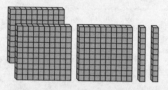

Hundreds	Tens	Ones

4. **Number Sense** Use the clues to solve the number puzzle.

I have a 5 in my ones place.
The digit in my tens place is 3 plus the digit in my ones place. The digit in my hundreds place is 2 less than the digit in my ones place. What number am I?

_____

5. **Higher Order Thinking** Look back at Item 4. Write your own place-value number puzzle. Give it to a friend to solve.

_____

_____

_____

_____

6. ✓**Assessment** Which number is shown?

Ⓐ 239

Ⓑ 329

Ⓒ 293

Ⓓ 339

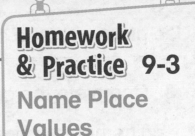

Another Look! You can find the value of each digit of a number by its place.

Hundreds	Tens	Ones
2	4	3

The value of the 2 is _2 hundreds_ or _200_ .

The value of the 4 is _4 tens_ or _40_ .

The value of the 3 is _3 ones_ or _3_ .

HOME ACTIVITY Choose two three-digit numbers. Ask your child to name the values of each digit in each number.

Use the number in the place-value chart. Write the value of each digit.

I.

Hundreds	Tens	Ones
8	2	1

The value of the 8 is _____ hundreds or _____ .

The value of the 2 is _____ tens or _____ .

The value of the I is _____ one or _____ .

2.

Hundreds	Tens	Ones
5	7	9

The value of the 5 is _____ hundreds or _____ .

The value of the 7 is _____ tens or _____ .

The value of the 9 is _____ ones or _____ .

Use place value to solve each problem.

3. Complete the chart to find the number.

The number has 0 ones.
It has 7 hundreds.
It has 8 tens.

Hundreds	Tens	Ones

What is the number? _____ .

4. Explain Stacy says the 4 in 643 has a value of 4 tens or 40. Do you agree with Stacy's reasoning? Explain. Use pictures, words, or numbers in your answer.

5. Higher Order Thinking Kayla wrote a three-digit number. The value of the digit in the hundreds place is 6 hundreds. The digit in the tens place is 3 less than the digit in the hundreds place. The sum of all three digits is 12. What is Kayla's number?

Kayla's number is _____ .

6. ✔Assessment What is the value of the 7 in the number 763?

Ⓐ 7

Ⓑ 70

Ⓒ 100

Ⓓ 700

Independent Practice

Use place-value blocks to count the hundreds, tens, and ones. Then show two other ways to make the number.

2.

Hundreds	Tens	Ones

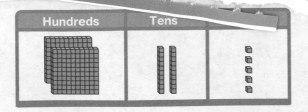

418 = _____

418 = _____

418 = _____

3.

Hundreds	Tens	Ones

163 = _____

163 = _____

163 = _____

4.

Hundreds	Tens	

225 = _____

225 = _____

225 = _____

Algebra Write the missing number.

5. $698 = 500 + \underline{\hspace{1cm}} + 8$

6. $939 = 900 + 20 + \underline{\hspace{1cm}}$

7. Carl made this model to show a number.

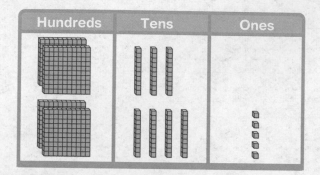

Hundreds	Tens	Ones

What number is shown? _____

Draw models to show another way Carl could make this number.

8. Explain Neha wants to make the same number in different ways. She says $300 + 130 + 9$ equals the same number as $500 + 30 + 9$. Do you agree with Neha? Explain.

_____

_____

_____

Remember, you can show the same number in different ways.

9. Higher Order Thinking Make 572 as hundreds, tens, and ones. Write as many ways as you can.

_____

_____

_____

10. ✅**Assessment** Which is a way to show 687? Choose all that apply.

☐ $600 + 70 + 17$

☐ $600 + 80 + 7$

☐ $600 + 180 + 7$

☐ $500 + 180 + 7$

Name _____

Another Look! You can show a number in different ways.

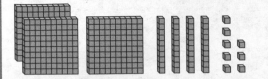

Remember that 10 tens makes 1 hundred. So, 1 hundred and 4 tens is the same as 14 tens.

HOME ACTIVITY Write the expanded form of a number and ask your child to tell you another way to show the number. For example, write $200 + 10 + 6$ or $900 + 40 + 3$.

__3__ hundreds, __4__ tens, and __8__ ones

$348 = \underline{300} + \underline{40} + \underline{8}$ is the same as

__2__ hundreds, __14__ tens, and __8__ ones

$348 = \underline{200} + \underline{140} + \underline{8}$

Show two different ways to name the number. You can use place-value blocks to help.

1. $734 = $ _____ hundreds, _____ tens, and _____ ones.

$734 = $ _____ + _____ + _____

$734 = $ _____ hundreds, _____ tens, and _____ ones.

$734 = $ _____ + _____ + _____

2. **Be Precise** What number does the model show?

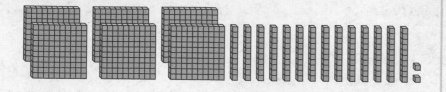

_____

3. **Number Sense** Write a three-digit number. Then write it in two different ways.

My Number _____

Way 1 _____

Way 2 _____

4. **Math and Science** Matt built a house with 164 blocks. The main part of his house has 100 blocks. The roof has 50 blocks. The chimney has 14 blocks. Write another way to use the same number of blocks for a new house.

Think about place value when you solve this problem.

5. **Higher Order Thinking** Write 936 two different ways using the charts.

Hundreds	Tens	Ones

Hundreds	Tens	Ones

6. ✅ **Assessment** Which is a way to show 764? Choose all that apply.

- ☐ 600 + 150 + 4
- ☐ 600 + 150 + 14
- ☐ 700 + 50 + 14
- ☐ 700 + 60 + 4

Name _____

Another Look! The digits in numbers can help you find patterns.

975	976	977	978	979	980
985	986	987	988	989	990
995	996	997	998	999	1,000

1,000 comes after 999.

Pick a row in the chart. Read the numbers across the row.

The ones digits go up by _____.

Pick a column in the chart and read the numbers from top to bottom.

The tens digits go up by _____.

HOME ACTIVITY Write a three-digit number such as 120. Ask your child to write four more numbers after it, counting by 1s. Then ask your child to start at the number and write four more numbers below it, counting by 10s.

Use place-value patterns and mental math to find the missing numbers.

1.

633		635		637	
	644			647	648
653			656	657	

2.

	285	286			289
294	295		297		299
304			307		

Topic 9 | Lesson 6

Digital Resources at SavvasRealize.com

Solve each problem.

3. Explain Manuel thinks the tens digit goes up by 1 in these numbers. Do you agree? Explain.

460, 470, 480, 490, 500, 510

_____

_____

_____

4. Explain Maribel thinks the tens digit goes up by 1 in these numbers. Do you agree? Explain.

864, 865, 866, 867, 868, 869

_____

_____

_____

5. Higher Order Thinking Write 5 three-digit numbers. From left to right, the ones digit in your numbers should go up by 1.

_____ , _____ , _____ , _____ , _____

Write 5 three-digit numbers. From left to right, the tens digit in your numbers should go up by 1.

_____ , _____ , _____ , _____ , _____

6. ✓Assessment Use the numbers on the cards. Write the missing numbers in the number chart.

| 557 | 539 | 545 | 547 |

535	536	537	538		540
	546		548	549	550
555	556		558	559	560

Name _____

Another Look! Skip count on the number line. Write the missing numbers.

We are skip counting by 10s!
160, 170, 180, 190...

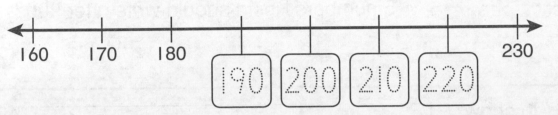

160   170   180   190   200   210   220   230

Find the difference between two given numbers that are next to each other. That tells you which number you are skip counting by.

HOME ACTIVITY Draw a number line with numbers that go up by 5s. Have your child tell you what number he or she can skip count by. Repeat this activity with numbers that go up by 10s.

Skip count on the number line. Write the missing numbers.

1.
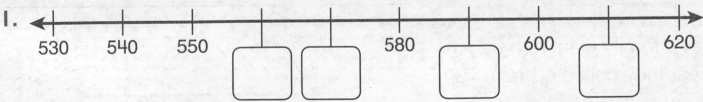

530   540   550   _____   _____   580   _____   600   _____   620

2.
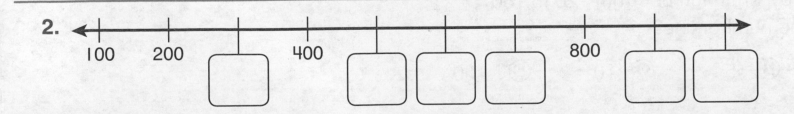

100   200   _____   400   _____   _____   _____   800   _____   _____

Solve the problems below.

3. **Look for Patterns** Bill wants to skip count by 10s from 710. He writes 710, 720, 730 on paper. What are the next 5 numbers Bill should write after 730?

_____ , _____ , _____ , _____ , _____

4. **Look for Patterns** Krista wants to skip count by 100s from 200. She writes 200, 300, 400 on paper. What are the next 5 numbers Krista should write after 400?

_____ , _____ , _____ , _____ , _____

5. **Higher Order Thinking** Linda wants to show skip counting by 5s from a number to get to 1,000. Write the numbers she should put on her number line below. How do you know?

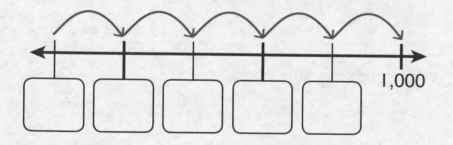

1,000

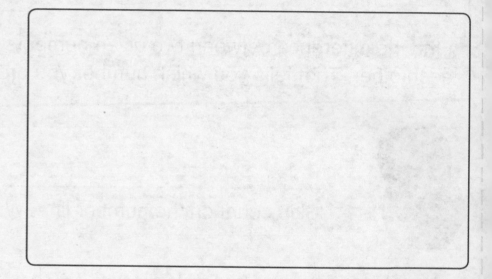

6. **✓Assessment** Izzy's family went to a beach 4 times. On their trips, they collected 120, 130, 140, and 150 shells.

Skip counting by what number from 120 to 150 is shown on the number line?

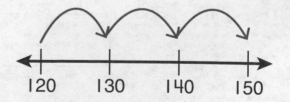

120   130   140   150

Ⓐ 2   Ⓑ 5   Ⓒ 10   Ⓓ 100

Independent Practice

Write a number to make each comparison correct. Draw a number line to help if needed.

7. 421 > _____

8. _____ < 884

9. 959 < _____

10. _____ < 8___

11. 103 = _____

12. 566 > _____

13. 394 < _____

14. _____ < 417

15. _____ > 789

Write <, >, or = to make each comparison correct.

16. 107 ◯ 106

17. 630 ◯ 629

18. 832 ◯ 832

19. Higher Order Thinking Write a number to make each comparison correct. Place the numbers on the number lines.

_____ < 780 < _____

_____ > 457 > _____

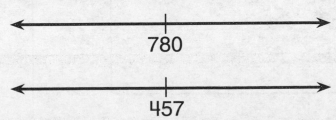

Problem Solving * Solve the problems below.

20. Reasoning Kim is thinking of a number.
It is greater than 447.
It is less than 635.
What could the number be?

_____

21. Reasoning Don is thinking of a number.
It is less than 982.
It is greater than 950.
What could the number be?

Think about how the numbers relate.

_____

22. Higher Order Thinking Monty picked a number card. The number is greater than 282. It is less than 284. What is the number? _____

Explain how you know.

_____

_____

_____

_____

23. ✅ **Assessment** What number is neither greater than nor less than the number shown? Explain how you know.

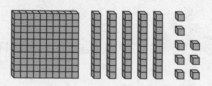

Topic 9 | Lesson 9

Name _____

Another Look! Think about the order of numbers.

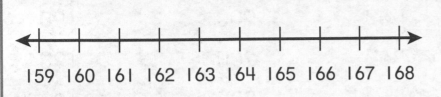

159 160 161 162 163 164 165 166 167 168

Numbers go on forever in both directions on a number line. So, 170 is also greater than 167.

HOME ACTIVITY Have your child choose a three-digit number. Then ask your child to name a number that is greater than that number and a number that is less than that number.

Write a number to make each comparison correct.

_160_ is **less than** 163.　　　_168_ is **greater than** 167.

_161_ is **greater than** 160 and **less than** 162.

Write a number to make each comparison correct. Use the number line to help you.

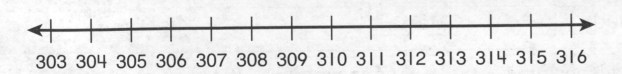

303 304 305 306 307 308 309 310 311 312 313 314 315 316

1. _____ is **less than** 304.

2. _____ is **greater than** 307.

3. _____ is **greater than** 314 and **less than** 316.

Generalize Write three different numbers to make each comparison correct. Draw a number line to help if needed.

4. 805 > _____ > 795

   805 > _____ > 795

   805 > _____ > 795

5. 457 < _____ < 462

   457 < _____ < 462

   457 < _____ < 462

6. 200 > _____ > 190

   200 > _____ > 190

   200 > _____ > 190

7. **Higher Order Thinking** Match each soccer player with a team number. Write the number in the box.

Team Numbers			
192	319	198	420

My number is greater than 197 and less than 199.

Carlos

My number is less than Carlos's number.

Jada

My number is less than 421 and greater than 419.

Marta

My number is greater than Carlos's number and less than Marta's number.

Jackson

8. ✓**Assessment** Which comparisons are correct? Choose all that apply.

☐ 294 < 293   ☐ 296 > 295

☐ 295 < 298   ☐ 297 = 297

9. ✓**Assessment** Write two numbers that are less than 909 and greater than 868. Explain how you know.

Name _____

Another Look! Sam needs to paint his taxi number on his taxi.

His number is the next greatest number in the pattern.

What is Sam's taxi number?

First sort the numbers from least to greatest.

405   415   410   400   ?

400 , 405 , 410 , 415

Then look for a pattern and name the pattern rule.

The hundreds digit stays the same. The numbers increase by 5 each time.

The pattern rule is increase by 5! Sam's taxi number is 420.

HOME ACTIVITY Write the numbers 285, 265, 255, 275, and 245 on small pieces of paper. Ask your child to sort the numbers from least to greatest. Then ask your child to tell you the pattern rule and to find the next number in the pattern.

Look for a number pattern to solve.

1. James wants to sort the numbers on his teddy bears from greatest to least. After he sorts the numbers, what number would come next?

666   676   686   656   ?

First sort the numbers from greatest to least.

_____, _____, _____, _____

Then look for a pattern and name the pattern rule.

_____

What number is next in the pattern? _____

Topic 9 | Lesson 10   Digital Resources at SavvasRealize.com   five hundred sixty-nine **569**

Bicycle Race

Jack and Sara join the purple team for the bike race. Their bike numbers will be the next two greater numbers in the pattern.

Help them find their bike numbers.

2. **Reasoning** List the bike numbers from least to greatest.

_____ , _____ , _____ , _____ , _____

3. **Look for Patterns** Look for a pattern and name the pattern rule. What are Jack's and Sara's bike numbers?

_____

_____

_____

_____

4. **Look for Patterns** Suppose new bike numbers are given in decreasing order. Then what numbers would Jack and Sara be given? Explain.

_____

_____

_____

Follow the Path

Color a path from **Start** to **Finish**. Follow the sums and differences that are even numbers. You can only move up, down, right, or left.

I can ...
add and subtract within 100.

Start								
66 − 28	15 + 12	64 − 27	57 + 36	99 − 66	53 − 14	23 + 46	75 − 22	52 + 13
15 + 35	59 − 28	57 + 22	87 − 74	56 − 12	78 − 52	61 + 15	42 − 29	29 + 16
53 + 43	44 + 39	90 − 18	47 − 23	61 + 39	61 − 36	24 + 38	15 + 58	73 − 52
85 − 39	56 + 17	43 − 11	25 + 26	81 − 28	61 + 14	53 − 37	33 + 38	45 − 18
33 + 57	78 − 52	56 + 12	87 − 32	16 + 45	93 − 24	63 + 15	26 + 44	27 − 19

Finish

A-Z Glossary

Word List
- compare
- decrease
- digits
- equals (=)
- expanded form
- greater than (>)
- hundred
- increase
- less than (<)
- ones
- place-value chart
- standard form
- tens
- thousand
- word form

Understand Vocabulary

Write *standard form*, *expanded form*, or *word form*.

1. 400 + 30 + 7

_____

2. four hundred thirty-seven

_____

3. 437

_____

Label each picture. Use terms from the Word List.

4.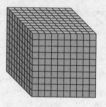

_____

5.

_____

6.

_____

Compare. Complete each sentence.

7. 901 is _____ 910.

8. 429 _____ 400 + 20 + 9.

Use Vocabulary in Writing

9. What is the next number in the pattern?

911, 921, 931, 941, _____

Explain how you solved the problem.
Use terms from the Word List.

_____

_____

_____

_____

Name _____

Set A

10 tens make 1 hundred.
You can count by hundreds.

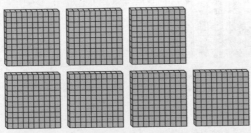

__700__ equals __7__ hundreds,

__0__ tens, and __0__ ones.

Complete the sentence.
Use models if needed.

1.

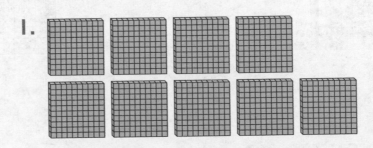

_____ equals _____ hundreds,

_____ tens, and _____ ones.

Set B

You can use place value to help
you write numbers.

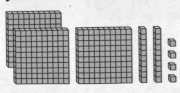

Hundreds	Tens	Ones
3	2	4

324

There are 3 hundreds, 2 tens,
and 4 ones in 324.

Write the numbers. Use models and
your workmat if needed.

2.

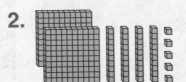

Hundreds	Tens	Ones

_____

3.

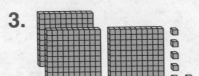

Hundreds	Tens	Ones

_____

You can write a number using the standard form, expanded form, and word form.

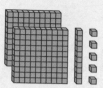

215

200 + 10 + 5

two hundred fifteen

Write the number in standard form, expanded form, and word form.

4.

_____

_____ + _____ + _____

_____

You can show different ways to make numbers.

Hundreds	Tens	Ones

238 = 200 + 30 + 8

238 = 200 + 20 + 18

238 = 230 + 8

Look at the models in the chart.
Show three different ways to make the number.

5.

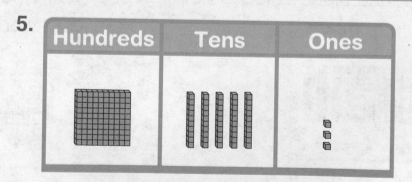

153 = _____ + _____ + _____

153 = _____ + _____ + _____

153 = _____ + _____

Name _____

Set E

You can look for patterns with numbers on a hundreds chart.

342	343	344	345	346	347
352	353	354	355	356	357
362	363	364	365	366	367

From left to right, the __ones__ digit goes up by 1.

From top to bottom, the __tens__ digit goes up by 1.

Use place-value patterns to find the missing numbers.

6.

574		576	577	578	
584		586		588	589
	595	596	597		

7.

	222		224	225	
	232		234	235	236
241	242		244		246

Set F

You can skip count by 5s, 10s, and 100s on a number line.

Skip count on the number line. Write the missing numbers.

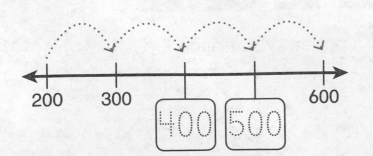

200   300   400   500   600

8.

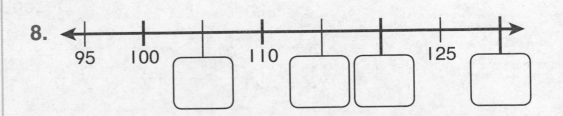

95   100   110   125

You can use place value to compare numbers.

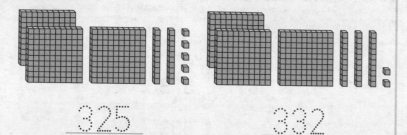

325   332

The hundreds are equal, so compare the tens. __20__ is less than __30__.

So, 325 ⊙< 332.

Compare each pair of numbers. Write >, <, or =.

9. 785 ◯ 793   10. 199 ◯ 198

11. 452 ◯ 452   12. 805 ◯ 810

13. 902 ◯ 897   14. 451 ◯ 516

15. 636 ◯ 629   16. 754 ◯ 754

Thinking Habits

Look for and Use Structure

Are there things in common that help me?

Is there a pattern? How does it help?

Look for a pattern to solve the problem.

17. These tags are in a drawer.

Describe a pattern you notice.

_____

_____

What is the missing number? _____

Name _____

9. Lee and Maria collect pennies.
Lee has 248 pennies.
Maria has 253 pennies.
Who has more pennies?

_____

Write >, <, or = to compare
the number of pennies.

248 ◯ 253

10. Jeff is thinking of a number.
The number has 2 hundreds.
It has more ones than tens.
It has 7 tens.

Which could be the number?
Choose all that apply.

☐ 276   ☐ 279

☐ 278   ☐ 289

11. Compare. Write >, < or =.

429 ◯ 294   849 ◯ 984

12. Write a number that makes the
comparison correct.

327 < ____   716 > ____

13. There are 367 girls and 326 boys at a school. Which is
the expanded form for the number of boys?

Ⓐ 200 + 30 + 6   Ⓑ 300 + 20 + 6   Ⓒ 300 + 60 + 2   Ⓓ 300 + 60 + 7

14. Which is a way to show 576? Choose all that apply.

☐ 500 + 60 + 16   ☐ 500 + 70 + 6   ☐ 500 + 6   ☐ 400 + 170 + 6

15. Use the numbers on the cards. Write the missing numbers in the number chart.

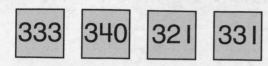

320		322	323	324
330		332		334
	341	342	343	344

16. Candy counts 405, 410, 415, 420, 425, 430. By what number does Candy skip count?

Ⓐ 2

Ⓑ 5

Ⓒ 10

Ⓓ 100

17. Skip count on the number line. Write the missing numbers.

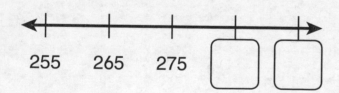

255   265   275

18. Is the statement true? Choose Yes or No.

576 < 675   ◯ Yes   ◯ No

435 > 354   ◯ Yes   ◯ No

698 < 896   ◯ Yes   ◯ No

899 < 799   ◯ Yes   ◯ No

Name _____

Reading Record
These students love to read!
These books show the number of pages
each student has read so far this year.

512 pages
Ken

493 pages
Luisa

427 pages
Ruth

378 pages
Tim

I. Write the number of pages Tim read
in expanded form.

_____ + _____ + _____

Write the number in word form.

2. Complete the place-value chart
to show the number of pages
Ruth read.

Hundreds	Tens	Ones

Show two other ways to write the number.

_____ + _____ + _____

_____ + _____ + _____

3. Show two ways to compare the number of pages
that Luisa read with the number of pages that
Ruth read. Use > and <.

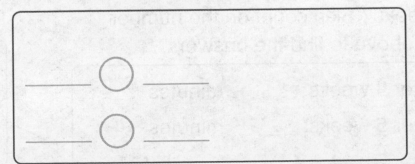

_____ ◯ _____

_____ ◯ _____

4. This number line shows the total number of minutes Diane read each week for 3 weeks.

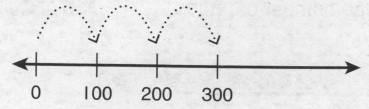

0   100   200   300

How many minutes did she read after the first week? _____ minutes

After the second week? _____ minutes

After the third week? _____ minutes

How many minutes did she read each week? Explain how you know.

5. Diane reads the same number of minutes each week. How many minutes does she read after 4 weeks? After 5 weeks? Skip count on the number line above to find the answers.

After 4 weeks: _____ minutes

After 5 weeks: _____ minutes

6. The table shows how many pages Jim read in three different months. If he follows the pattern, how many pages will Jim read in April and May?

Number of Pages Read	
January	210
February	220
March	230
April	?
May	?

Part A
What pattern do you see in the table?

Part B
How many pages will Jim read in April and May?

Topic 9 | Performance Assessment

TOPIC 10

Add Within 1,000 Using Models and Strategies

Essential Question: What are strategies for adding numbers to 1,000?

Look at all the tall buildings!

It takes a lot of planning to build a tall building. Would you like to try?

Wow! Let's do this project and learn more.

Math and Science Project: Building Up to 1,000

Find Out Use spaghetti sticks and mini marshmallows. The total for both cannot be more than 1,000. First, decide how many of each to use. Then share. Build the tallest buildings you can.

Journal: Make a Book Describe your building in a book. In your book, also:

- Tell how many spaghetti sticks and mini marshmallows you used.

- Tell how you would make a better building if you did it again.

Digital Resources

Solve   Learn   Glossary

Tools   Assessment   Help   Games

Name _____

Review What You Know

1. Circle all of the **hundreds digits** in the numbers below.

5 0 2

5 8

1,0 0 0

2. Write the **expanded form** of the number.

846

_____

3. Write the **word form** of the number.

265

_____

_____

Open Number Lines

4. Use the open number line to find the sum.

54 + 13 = _____

Mental Math

5. Use mental math to find each sum.

40 + 37 = _____

6 + 77 + 4 = _____

Partial Sums

6. Use partial sums to add.

```
  4 6        2 9
+ 5 3      + 6 1
-----      -----
```

584 five hundred eighty-four

Name _____

Another Look! Use mental math to add 10 or 100 to three-digit numbers.
Find $315 + 10$ and $315 + 100$.

 plus 10
plus 100

The tens digit goes up by 1 when you add 10.

$315 + 10 = 3\boxed{2}5$

The hundreds digit goes up by 1 when you add 100.

$315 + 100 = \boxed{4}15$

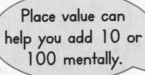 Place value can help you add 10 or 100 mentally.

HOME ACTIVITY Choose a number between 200 and 300. Ask your child to add 10 to the number and tell you the sum. Repeat with adding 100 to the number.

 Add using mental math. Use models if needed.

1. 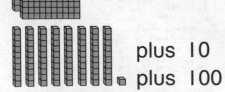 plus 10
plus 100

_____ + 10 = _____

_____ + 100 = _____

2. 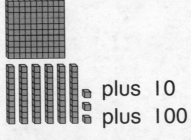 plus 10
plus 100

_____ + 10 = _____

_____ + 100 = _____

3. 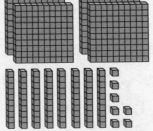 plus 10
plus 100

_____ + 10 = _____

_____ + 100 = _____

Look for Patterns Use mental math. Write the missing digit.

4. $100 + \boxed{}00 = 200$

5. $223 + \boxed{}00 = 323$

6. $10 + 351 = 3\boxed{}1$

A-Z Vocabulary Use mental math. Write the missing digit.
Then complete the sentence with **addend** or **sum**.

7. $6\boxed{}3 + 10 = 683$

683 is the _____.

8. $\boxed{}35 + 100 = 535$

The _____ is 535.

9. $802 + 10 = 81\boxed{}$

802 is an _____.

Higher Order Thinking Write the missing digits.

10. $22\boxed{} + 100 + 105 = 4\boxed{}8$

11. $\boxed{}12 + 205 + 10 = 32\boxed{}$

Use mental math to solve.

12. ✓**Assessment** Tanner has 679 stamps.
She has 669 stamps in her album.
How many stamps are **NOT** in her album?

Ⓐ 10

Ⓒ 100

Ⓑ 20

Ⓓ 689

13. ✓**Assessment** Darrin has 274 basketball
stickers and 100 football stickers.
How many sports stickers does he have?

Ⓐ 174

Ⓒ 284

Ⓑ 184

Ⓓ 374

590 five hundred ninety

Topic 10 | Lesson 1

Independent Practice ☆   Use an open number line to find each sum.

3. 278 + 152 = _____

4. 637 + 242 = _____

5. 197 + 523 = _____

6. 202 + 598 = _____

7. **Higher Order Thinking** Lisa finds 550 + 298 using the open number line below.
Is her work correct? Explain.

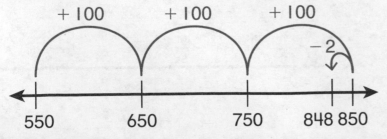

8. **Reason** Jose has 181 cards. He collects 132 more. How many cards does he have now?

_____ cards

9. **A-Z** **Vocabulary** Complete the sentence using two of these terms.

      add **tens** **open number line** **rule**

An _____

can be used to

_____ .

10. **Higher Order Thinking** Use open number lines to find $446 + 215$ in two different ways.

$446 + 215 =$ _____

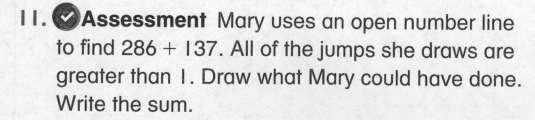

11. ✓**Assessment** Mary uses an open number line to find $286 + 137$. All of the jumps she draws are greater than 1. Draw what Mary could have done. Write the sum.

$286 + 137 =$ _____

Name _____

   Help Tools Games

Another Look! Find 284 + 231.

I can add by 100s, 10s, and 1s or make bigger jumps to find 284 + 231.

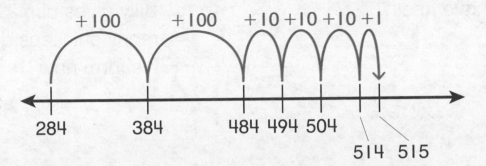

Way 1:

+100   +100   +10 +10 +10 +1

284   384   484 494 504

514 515

HOME ACTIVITY Ask your child to show how he or she would find 153 + 162 using an open number line.

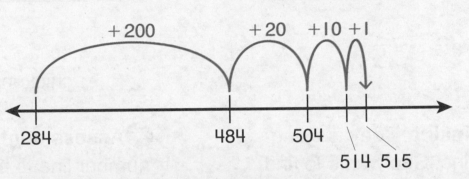

Way 2:

+200   +20 +10 +1

284   484   504

514 515

Use an open number line to find each sum.

1. 483 + 172 = _____

2. 288 + 324 = _____

← ——————————— →   ← ——————————— →

Solve each problem. Use the number line to show your work.

3. **Reasoning** Jeb has 264 blocks in a box. Mia gives Jeb 341 more blocks. How many blocks does Jeb have in all?

_____ blocks

4. Josh has 509 chickens on his farm. Bob gives Josh 111 chickens, and Billy gives him 21 chickens. How many chickens does Josh have on his farm now?

_____ chickens

5. **Higher Order Thinking** Zoey is using an open number line. She wants to find 232 + 578. Which addend should she place on the number line to start? Explain.

_____

_____

_____

6. ✅ **Assessment** John uses an open number line to find 570 + 241. One of his jumps is + 40. Draw what John could have done. Write the sum.

570 + 241 = _____

Topic 10 | Lesson 2

Name _____

Another Look! Use any strategy to find 358 + 213.

One Way You can add the hundreds, the tens, and the ones.

Add hundreds.	Add tens.	Add ones.
300	50	8
+ 200	+ 10	+ 3
500	60	11

Or you can use easier numbers to find 358 + 213.

Add the partial sums.
$500 + 60 + 11 = 571$

So, $358 + 213 = \underline{571}$.

Another Way

358 is $360 - 2$.

$360 + 213 = 573$

Take away 2.

$573 - 2 = 571$

HOME ACTIVITY Ask your child to show you how to add 305 + 497. Have your child explain how he or she does the addition.

Use any strategy to solve each problem. Show your work.

1. $248 + 455 = $ _____

2. $209 + 376 = $ _____

3. $597 + 122 = $ _____

Algebra Write each missing number.

4. $285 + 507 =$ _____

5. _____ $= 378 + 142$

6. $802 =$ _____ $+ 431$

Be Precise Find the total number of buttons for each.
Use the chart. Add any way you choose.

Button	Number
animal	378
sport	142
fruit	296
holiday	455

7. Mrs. Jones buys all of the animal and fruit buttons.

_____ + _____ = _____

_____ buttons

8. Mr. Frost buys all of the sport and holiday buttons.

_____ + _____ = _____

_____ buttons

Are you using numbers and symbols correctly?

---

9. **Higher Order Thinking** A theater wants to add 140 seats. Then the theater will have a total of 375 seats. How many seats does the theater have now?

_____ seats

10. **Assessment** Rob has 225 marbles. Jake has 69 more marbles than Rob. How many marbles do they have in all?

294   509   519   529

Ⓐ   Ⓑ   Ⓒ   Ⓓ

Name _____

Another Look! You can use place value to add 2 three-digit numbers.

$164 + 253 = $ __?__

Find the partial sums. Then add the partial sums to find the sum.

Hundreds	Tens	Ones

HOME ACTIVITY Write $581 + 294$ on a sheet of paper. Ask your child to use partial sums to find the sum.

1. Add the hundreds.
2. Add the tens.
3. Add the ones.
4. Add the partial sums.

Hundreds	Tens	Ones
1	6	4
+ 2	5	3
3	0	0
1	1	0
		7
4	1	7

So, $164 + 253 = $ __417__.

Add. Use partial sums. Show your work. Use place-value blocks if needed.

1. $218 + 136$

Hundreds	Tens	Ones
2	1	8
+ 1	3	6
Hundreds: 3	0	0
Tens:	4	0
Ones:	1	4
Sum =		

2. $365 + 248$

Hundreds	Tens	Ones
3	6	5
+ 2	4	8
Hundreds:		
Tens:		
Ones:		
Sum =		

3.   7 1 4
     + 1 3 5

4.   1 6 8
     + 4 2 3

5.   2 6 6
     + 5 9 2

6.   4 7 4
     + 2 3 8

7.   5 6 7
     + 1 3 7

---

8. **Higher Order Thinking** Fill in the missing numbers to make the addition problem true.

	Hundreds	Tens	Ones
	2	☐	8
+	☐	7	☐
Hundreds:	☐	0	0
Tens:		☐	0
Ones:		☐	☐
Sum =	8	9	0

9. ✓**Assessment** Which is the same amount as 462 + 253? Choose Yes or No.

600 + 11 + 5   ○ Yes ○ No

600 + 110 + 5   ○ Yes ○ No

600 + 100 + 15   ○ Yes ○ No

715   ○ Yes ○ No

There is more than one way to write a sum.

Tools   Assessment

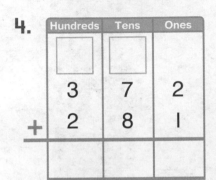 **Independent Practice** Add. Draw place-value blocks to show your work. Regroup if needed.

4.

Hundreds	Tens	Ones
3	7	2
+ 2	8	1

Hundreds	Tens	Ones

5.

Hundreds	Tens	Ones
3	4	9
+ 1	8	2

Hundreds	Tens	Ones

6.

Hundreds	Tens	Ones
2	7	3
+ 2	5	9

Hundreds	Tens	Ones

7. Higher Order Thinking Ben said that the sum of 157 and 197 is 254. Nikki said that Ben made a mistake. Who is correct? Explain.

Add 157 and 197. Do you get the same sum as Ben?

_____

_____

Solve each problem below.
You can use models to help.

You can use or draw place-value blocks to model the problem.

8. **Model** On Friday, 354 people went to the fair. On Saturday, 551 people went to the fair.

   How many people went to the fair in all?

Hundreds	Tens	Ones
☐	☐	
+		

_____ people

9. **Higher Order Thinking** Write an addition problem that shows regrouping both the ones and the tens. Use 3-digit numbers between 100 and 400 as addends. Find the sum.

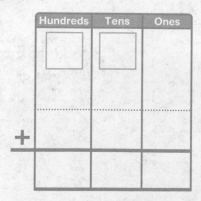

Hundreds	Tens	Ones
☐	☐	
+		

10. ✓**Assessment** Use the numbers on the cards. Write the missing digits in each sum.

6	1	4	7

   ```
     1 6 9          4 4 8
   + 4 7 5        + 3 2 3
   ─────────      ─────────
   ☐ ☐ 4          7 ☐ ☐
   ```

Topic 10 | Lesson 5

Another Look! You can follow these steps to add three-digit numbers.

Step 1: Add the ones. Regroup if needed.
Step 2: Add the tens. Regroup if needed.
Step 3: Add the hundreds.

5 + 8 = 13 ones.
Regroup 10 ones for 1 ten.

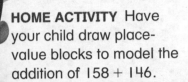

HOME ACTIVITY Have your child draw place-value blocks to model the addition of 158 + 146.

Hundreds	Tens	Ones
135		
248		

135 + 248 = 383

Add. Regroup if needed. Draw models to help.

1. 341 + 127 = _____

Hundreds	Tens	Ones

2. 524 + 249 = _____

Hundreds	Tens	Ones

Add. Look for the pattern.

Look for Patterns Write and solve the next addition problem that follows each pattern.

3.

Hundreds	Tens	Ones
2	0	9
+ 1	2	3

Hundreds	Tens	Ones
3	0	9
+ 2	2	3

Hundreds	Tens	Ones
4	0	9
+ 3	2	3

Hundreds	Tens	Ones
+		

Look for patterns in the addends and the sums.

4.

Hundreds	Tens	Ones
3	1	5
+ 4	2	7

Hundreds	Tens	Ones
4	1	5
+ 3	2	7

Hundreds	Tens	Ones
5	1	5
+ 2	2	7

Hundreds	Tens	Ones
+		

5. **Higher Order Thinking** Write and solve an addition story for 482 + 336.

_____

_____

_____

_____

6. ✓**Assessment** Use the numbers on the cards. Write the missing digits in each sum.

1	8	6	4

```
  2 3 5
+ 1 8 2
□ □ 7
```

```
  6 5 2
+ 2 1 6
8 □ □
```

Topic 10 | Lesson 5

Solve & Share

Find 375 + 235. Explain your strategy.

I can ...
use different addition strategies and explain why they work.

I can also model with math.

Lauren, Nate, and Josh use different ways to find 257 + 126.

Lauren uses an open number line. She starts at 257 and mentally adds up the hundreds, the tens, and the ones.

Lauren's Number Line

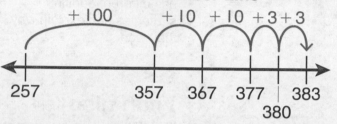

+100   +10 +10 +3 +3

257   357   367   377 | 383
                          380

Nate draws place-value blocks. He regroups 10 ones as 1 ten.

Nate's Place-Value Blocks

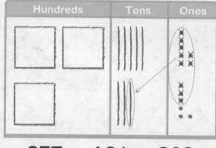

| Hundreds | Tens | Ones |

257 + 126 = 383

Josh uses place value to write the addends in a column. He regroups 10 ones as 1 ten.

Josh's Addition

```
   1
  257
+ 126
-----
  383
```

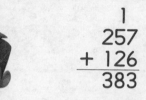

Why does each of these strategies work?

Do You Understand?

Show Me! Choose a strategy shown above. Explain how it works.

☆ Guided Practice ☆

Choose any strategy to solve the problem. Show your work. Then explain your work.

1. 624 + 248 = <u>872</u>

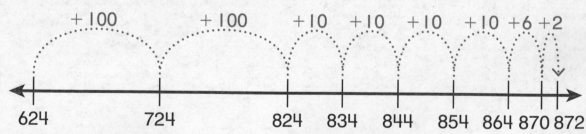

+100   +100   +10 +10 +10 +10 +6 +2

624   724   824 834 844 854 864 870 872

Start at 624. Add 2 hundreds. Then add 4 tens. Count on 6 to get to 870, then add 2 more to reach 872. The jumps add up to 248.

Independent Practice

Choose any strategy to solve each addition problem. Show your work. Then explain.

2. 212 + 487 = _____

_____

_____

3. 874 + 109 = _____

_____

_____

4. 419 + 532 = _____

_____

_____

5. 650 + 270 = _____

How many different ways can you use?

_____

Problem Solving

Solve each problem any way you choose.
Show your work.

6. **Reasoning** Lee School needs 407 folders for its students. Jefferson School needs 321 folders for its students. How many folders do both schools need?

_____ folders

7. **Reasoning** There are 229 people at the football game. 108 more people arrive at the game. How many people are at the football game now?

_____ people

8. **Higher Order Thinking** Tommy found 125 + 598. Since 598 is close to 600, he added 125 + 600 = 725. Then he subtracted 2 to get 723.

Why did Tommy subtract 2? Explain.

9. ✓**Assessment** There are 192 ants on an ant farm. 397 more ants join the ant farm. How many ants are on the ant farm now?

Use the number line to solve. Explain.

Copyright © Savvas Learning Company LLC. All Rights Reserved.

Name _____

Another Look! Find $219 + 468$.

One Way

You can use mental math and an open number line to keep track of your thinking.

You can add numbers in any order.

You can start with 468 and add 219.

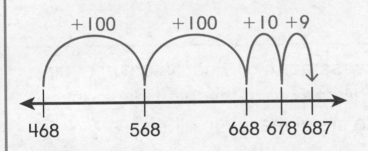

+100   +100   +10 +9

468   568   668 678 687

Another Way

You can also use paper and pencil to find the sum. Regroup if you need to.

$$\begin{array}{r} 1 \\ 219 \\ + 468 \\ \hline 687 \end{array}$$

To add 9, think add 10. Then subtract 1.

HOME ACTIVITY Ask your child to explain how to solve $429 + 378$.

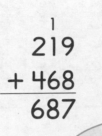

Choose any strategy to solve the addition problem. Show your work. Then explain your work.

1. $192 + 587 =$ _____

2. $269 + 658 =$ _____

_____

_____

Topic 10 | Lesson 6

Digital Resources at SavvasRealize.com

six hundred nineteen **619**

Reasoning Choose any strategy to solve the addition problem. Show your work. Then explain your work.

3. 635 + 284 = _____

_____

_____

4. 701 + 103 = _____

_____

_____

5. **Higher Order Thinking** Explain TWO different ways to find 562 + 399.

One Way

Another Way

6. ✓**Assessment** 519 adults are at a fair. 369 children are at the fair. How many people are at the fair in all?

Use the number line to solve. Explain.

⟵————————————————⟶

_____

_____

_____

Name _____

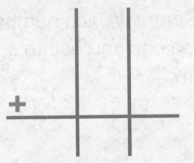
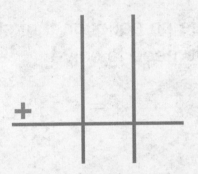

Independent Practice ☆ Solve each problem.

7. Write a problem where you need to regroup to make a ten or a hundred. Each addend must be three digits. Solve your problem. Then explain why you needed to regroup.

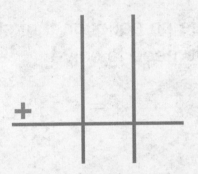

_____

_____

_____

_____

8. Write a problem where you do not need to regroup to make a ten or a hundred. Each addend must be three digits. Solve your problem. Then explain why you don't need to regroup.

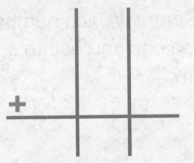

_____

_____

_____

_____

Tickets Sold

The table shows how many tickets were sold at a theater.

How many tickets were sold on Thursday and Saturday?

TICKETS

25145843 25145843

Tickets Sold	
Thursday	198
Friday	245
Saturday	367

9. **Make Sense** Which numbers and operation can you use to solve the problem?

_____

_____

_____

10. **Model** Write an equation that shows the problem you need to solve.

_____ ◯ _____ = _____

11. **Generalize** Use what you know about adding 3-digit numbers to solve the problem. Explain what you did.

_____

_____

_____

_____

Find a partner. Get paper and a pencil. Each partner chooses a different color: light blue or dark blue.

Partner 1 and Partner 2 each point to a black number at the same time. Both partners subtract Partner 2's number from Partner 1's number.

If the answer is on your color, you get a tally mark. Work until one partner gets seven tally marks.

I can ...
subtract within 100.

Partner 1							Partner 2
	53	19	43	62	37	30	
59							45
78	48	65	81	32	51	76	27
92	14	71	58	66	48	25	16
82	44	37	55	47	33	67	11
64							34

Tally Marks for Partner 1

Tally Marks for Partner 2

A-Z Glossary

Word List
- addend
- break apart
- digits
- hundreds
- mental math
- open number line
- partial sum
- sum

Understand Vocabulary

Choose a term from the Word List to complete each sentence.

1. When adding 193 + 564, the sum of 90 + 60 is called a

_____.

2. In 709 + 187, 709 is an _____.

3. You can use an _____ to count on.

---

4. In 841, there are

_____ hundreds.

5. Give the value of each digit in 610.

_____

6. Use mental math to find 198 + 362.

_____

Use Vocabulary in Writing

7. Use words to tell how to find 249 + 201. Use terms from the Word List.

_____
_____
_____
_____
_____

Name _____

Set A

You can use mental math to add 10 or 100 to a number.

$362 + 10 = ?$

The tens digit goes up by 1.

$362 + 10 = 372$

$362 + 100 = ?$

The hundreds digit goes up by 1.

$362 + 100 = 462$

Add using mental math.

1. $600 + 10 \ =$ _____

$600 + 100 =$ _____

2. $543 + 10 \ =$ _____

$543 + 100 =$ _____

3. $799 + 10 \ =$ _____

$799 + 100 =$ _____

Set B

You can use an open number line to add. Find $327 + 126$.

First, place 327 on the line.

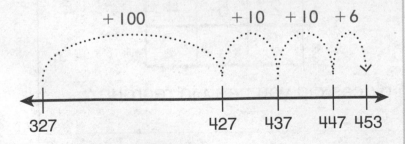

Count on by 100s, 10s, and 6 more on the line.

So, $327 + 126 =$ _453_ .

Use an open number line to find each sum.

4. $594 + 132 =$ _____

5. $157 + 245 =$ _____

You can draw place-value blocks to show addition. Find $163 + 144$.

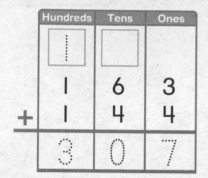

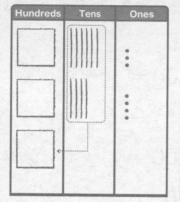

Add. Regroup and draw models if needed.

6.

Hundreds	Tens	Ones
4	0	8
+ 3	2	6

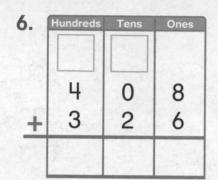

7.

Hundreds	Tens	Ones
2	2	5
+ 3	6	1

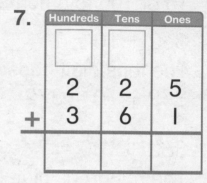

Thinking Habits

Repeated Reasoning

What can I use from one problem to help with another problem?

Are there things that repeat?

Solve the problem. Use repeated reasoning.

8.

Find the sum.

Hundreds	Tens	Ones
5	6	8
+ 2	5	4

Which places did you need to regroup?

_____

How does regrouping work?

_____

_____

630 six hundred thirty

Topic 10 | Reteaching

1. Emily has 100 sun stickers. She has 382 star stickers and 10 moon stickers. How many sun and star stickers does Emily have?

Ⓐ 492   Ⓒ 393

Ⓑ 482   Ⓓ 392

2. Tyrone collects baseball cards. He gives 138 cards to his friend. Now he has 428 cards. How many baseball cards did Tyrone have before he gave some away?

Ⓐ 290   Ⓒ 556

Ⓑ 550   Ⓓ 566

3. Use the open number line to solve the problem. Write the missing numbers in the boxes.

$421 + 250 = ?$

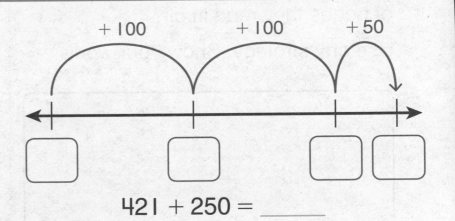

$421 + 250 = \underline{\hspace{2cm}}$

4. Which is the same amount as $528 + 167$? Choose all that apply.

☐ $500 + 80 + 15$ ☐ $500 + 180 + 15$ ☐ $600 + 90 + 5$ ☐ $600 + 80 + 15$

5. Is the sum equal to 488? Choose Yes or No.

$478 + 10 = ?$ $388 + 100 = ?$ $248 + 240 = ?$ $188 + 300 = ?$

○ Yes ○ No   ○ Yes ○ No   ○ Yes ○ No   ○ Yes ○ No

6. Rich has 335 pennies.
Beth has 58 more pennies than Rich.
How many pennies do they have in all?

(A) 277

(B) 393

(C) 628

(D) 728

7. Use the numbers on the cards.
Write the missing digits.

| 2 | 3 | 6 | 7 |

```
  4 7 2          4 3 4
+ 2 5 6        + 2 5 9
───────        ───────
 ☐ ☐ 8          ☐ 9 ☐
```

8. Molly reads 184 pages. Pat reads
294 pages. What is the total number
of pages they read in all?

Use any strategy. Show your work.

_____ pages

9. On Saturday, 449 people visit the zoo.
On Sunday, 423 people visit the zoo.
How many people visit the zoo in all?

Use the open number line to solve.
Explain your work.

Name _____

Recycling Race

Westbrook School is having a recycling contest. The table shows the number of cans each grade collected in February.

Cans Collected in February	
First grade	264
Second grade	302
Third grade	392
Fourth grade	425

1. How many cans did the first-grade students and the second-grade students collect in all?
Use the open number line to solve.

_____ cans

2. Bruce used partial sums to find how many cans the third-grade students and fourth-grade students collected in all.

$$392$$
$$+\ 425$$

Hundreds: 700
Tens: 11
Ones: +   7
             718

Do you agree with his answer?
Circle **yes**   or   **no**.

Explain your answer.

3. Which two grades collected a total of 689 cans? Choose any strategy to solve the problem. Show your work. Explain which strategy you used.

The _____ grade and the _____ grade collected a total of 689 cans.

Here are some addition strategies you have learned.

Addition Strategies

Open Number Line   Partial Sums
Compensation   Place-value Blocks
Mental Math   Regrouping
Break apart numbers

4. The second-grade students collected 432 cans in March. They collected 198 cans in April. Tom and Bill each add to find how many cans the class collected in all. One of them checks his work and finds the correct sum.

Tom's Way	Bill's Way
11	
432	432
+ 198	+ 198
630	520

Who added correctly? Explain.

Who answered incorrectly? What did he do wrong?

Topic 10 | Performance Assessment

TOPIC 11
Subtract Within 1,000 Using Models and Strategies

Essential Question: What are strategies for subtracting numbers to 1,000?

Bees help move pollen from one flower to another!

Moving the pollen helps plants grow fruit and vegetables.

Wow! Let's do this project and learn more.

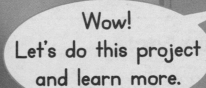

Math and Science Project: Making Models

Find Out Use a paintbrush as a model of a bee's leg. Dip the brush in a bowl of sugar. Then dip the brush in a bowl of pepper. Take turns. What happens to the sugar? What happens to the pepper?

Journal: Make a Book Show what you learn in a book. In your book, also:

- Tell how bees help move pollen between plants.

- Show how to use a model to help subtract three-digit numbers.

Name _____

Review What You Know

A-Z Vocabulary

1. Circle each number that is **less than** 607.

598

608

706

2. Circle each number that is **greater than** 299.

352

300

298

3. Circle the group of numbers that **decrease** by 100 from left to right.

650, 550, 450, 350

320, 420, 520, 620

570, 560, 550, 540

Subtraction Facts

4. Write each difference.

$$14 \quad 11 \quad 16$$
$$-7 \quad -4 \quad -9$$

Think of addition facts to help.

Regrouping

5. Use regrouping to find the difference. Be ready to explain your work.

$$54$$
$$-29$$

Math Story

6. Ben has 64 comic books. He gives 36 comic books to friends. How many comic books does Ben have left?

_____ comic books

Independent Practice   Subtract using mental math. Use models if needed.

5. 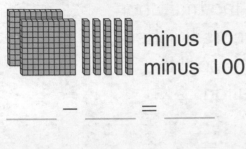 minus 10
minus 100

___ − ___ = ___

___ − ___ = ___

6. 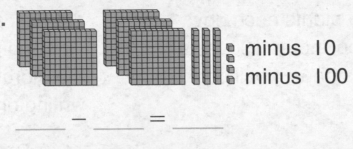 minus 10
minus 100

___ − ___ = ___

___ − ___ = ___

7. 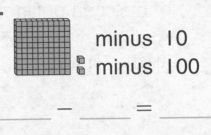 minus 10
minus 100

___ − ___ = ___

___ − ___ = ___

8. 719 − 10 = _____

9. 400 − 100 = _____

10. 308 − 10 = _____

11. 520 − 100 = _____

12. 975 − 10 = _____

13. 143 − 100 = _____

Algebra Find the missing numbers. Use mental math to solve.

14. 362 − ☐ = 352

15. 801 − ☐ = 701

16. 449 = 549 − ☐

17. 657 − ☐ = 647

18. 215 − ☐ = 205

19. 700 − ☐ = 690

20. **Math and Science** Marni is studying facts about bees. She finds that one type of bee can pollinate 955 plants each day. A different type of bee pollinates 100 fewer plants. How many plants does it pollinate?

_____ − _____ = _____

_____ plants

21. **Model** There was a marathon in Dundee. 10 of the runners did **NOT** finish the marathon. How many runners finished the marathon? Model by writing an equation.

DUNDEE MARATHON
689 RUNNERS

_____ − _____ = _____

_____ runners

22. **Higher Order Thinking** Think of a 3-digit number. Write a story about subtracting 100 from your number. Then complete the equation to show your subtraction.

_____ − _____ = _____

23. ✓**Assessment** Which is equal to 100 less than 463? Choose all that apply.

☐ 363

☐ 300 + 60 + 3

☐ 563

☐ 500 + 60 + 3

Topic 11 | Lesson 1

Help Tools Games

Another Look! Use mental math to subtract 10 or 100 from 3-digit numbers.

Find 278 − 10 and 278 − 100.

 minus 10
minus 100

Place value can help you subtract 10 or 100 mentally.

HOME ACTIVITY Choose a number between 300 and 400. Ask your child to subtract 10 from the number and tell you the difference. Repeat with subtracting 100 from the same number.

The tens digit goes down by 1 when you subtract 278 − 10.

278 − 10 = 2 6 8

The hundreds digit goes down by 1 when you subtract 278 − 100.

278 − 100 = ☐ 78

 Subtract using mental math. Use models if needed.

1. 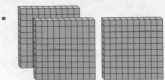 minus 10
minus 100

_____ − 10 = _____

_____ − 100 = _____

2. minus 10
minus 100

_____ − 10 = _____

_____ − 100 = _____

3. minus 10
minus 100

_____ − 10 = _____

_____ − 100 = _____

Look for Patterns Use mental math. Write the missing digit.

4. $\boxed{}69 - 100 = 469$

5. $\boxed{}00 - 10 = 790$

6. $402 - 10 = 3\boxed{}2$

A-Z Vocabulary Use mental math. Write the missing digit. Then complete the sentence with **greater than** or **less than**.

7. $271 - 100 = 1\boxed{}1$

171 is 100 _____ 271.

8. $475 - 100 = \boxed{}75$

475 is 100 _____ 375.

9. $612 - \boxed{}0 = 602$

602 is ten _____ 612.

---

10. **Higher Order Thinking** Adam is subtracting $708 - 10$ mentally. He thinks the tens digit and the hundreds digit will change. He gets 698 for his answer. Is Adam's thinking correct? Explain.

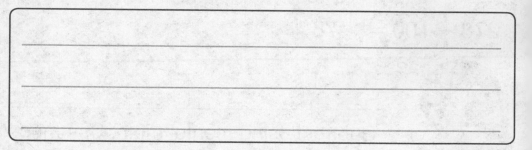

Use mental math to solve each story problem.

11. ✓**Assessment** There are 287 animal crackers in a box. Some second graders eat 100 of the crackers. How many crackers have **NOT** been eaten?

   Ⓐ 387   Ⓒ 187

   Ⓑ 277   Ⓓ 87

12. ✓**Assessment** Which is equal to 10 less than 145? Choose all that apply.

   ☐ 135   ☐ 155

   ☐ $100 + 30 + 5$ ☐ $100 + 50 + 5$

Name _____

☆ Independent Practice ☆   Use an open number line to find each difference.

3. 451 − 132 = _____

4. 735 − 242 = _____

5. 873 − 225 = _____

6. 492 − 314 = _____

7. **Higher Order Thinking** Show two different ways
to find 680 − 237. Use the open number lines.

680 − 237 = _____

8. **Model** There are 541 raffle tickets to sell. The second grade class sells 212 raffle tickets. How many raffle tickets are left to sell?

_____ raffle tickets

9. **Model** Fran has 712 stamps. Bill has 137 fewer stamps than Fran. How many stamps does Bill have?

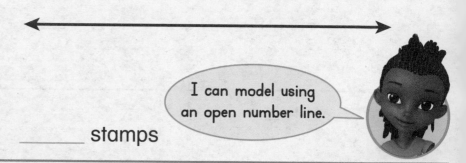

I can model using an open number line.

_____ stamps

10. **Higher Order Thinking** Count back on the number line to find 962 − 233. Write how many hundreds, tens, and ones you counted back. Then write the equation.

I counted back _____ hundreds, _____ tens, and _____ ones.

_____ ◯ _____ = _____

11. ✅ **Assessment** The open number line below shows a subtraction problem. Complete the equation. Write the numbers that are used to subtract and the difference.

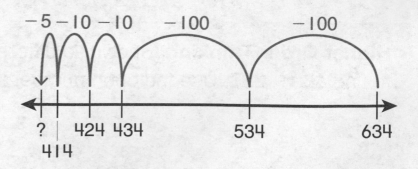

−5 −10 −10   −100   −100

? | 424 434   534   634
414

_____ − _____ = _____

Help   Tools   Games

Another Look! Find 917 − 322.

Here is one way.

I can count back by 100s, 10s, and 1s or make bigger jumps to find 917 − 322.

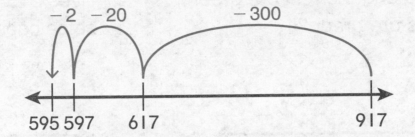

-2 -20 -300

595 597   617   917

So, 917 − 322 = 595

HOME ACTIVITY Tell your child to find 445 − 152 using an open number line.

Use an open number line to find each difference.

1. 925 − 230 = _____

2. 384 − 126 = _____

Solve each problem using an open number line.

3. **Model** 464 grapes are in a basket. 126 of the grapes are red and the rest are green. How many grapes are green?

_____ green grapes

4. **Model** Gabby has 592 bottle caps. She gives 215 bottle caps to Leroy. How many bottle caps does Gabby have left?

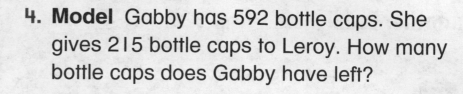

_____ bottle caps

5. **Higher Order Thinking** Write a math story for 348 − 144. Draw an open number line to solve the problem.

_____

_____

_____

_____

$348 - 144 =$ _____

6. ✅**Assessment** The open number line below shows a subtraction problem. Complete the equation. Write the numbers that are used to subtract and the difference.

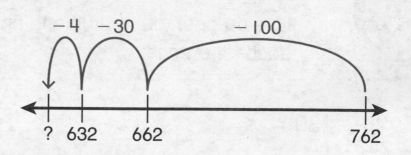

_____ − _____ = _____

Tools Assessment

Independent Practice

Add up on the open number line to find each difference.
Then add to check your work.

3. 530 − 318 = _____

_____ + _____ = _____

4. 735 − 429 = _____

_____ + _____ = _____

5. 802 − 688 = _____

_____ + _____ = _____

6. **A-Z** **Vocabulary** Complete the sentences using each word below once.

ones   **add**   **number**

You can add up to subtract on an open number line.

Start at the _____ you are subtracting.

_____ up hundreds, tens, and

_____ .

Stop at the number you subtract from.

7. Reasoning Yun has 780 blocks. Marsha has 545 fewer blocks than Yun. How many blocks does Marsha have?

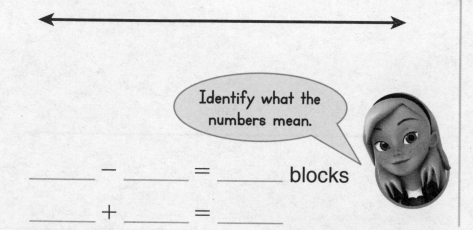

Identify what the numbers mean.

_____ − _____ = _____ blocks

_____ + _____ = _____

8. Higher Order Thinking Vic wants to find 463 − 258 on an open number line. Should he count back or add up? Explain.

9. ✓Assessment Write a math story for 653 − 529. Add up on the open number line to solve. Add to check your work.

_____ − _____ = _____

_____ + _____ = _____

Name _____

Another Look! Find $664 - 450$.

Here is one way.

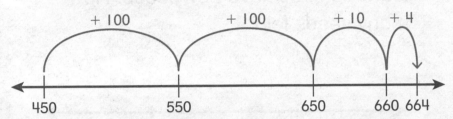

+100   +100   +10   +4

450   550   650   660 664

I can add up to subtract! So, $664 - 450 = 214$.

Check: $214 + 450 = 664$

Add hundreds, tens, and ones. $100 + 100 + 10 + 4 = 214$

HOME ACTIVITY Have your child add up to subtract $873 - 659$ on an open number line. Then have your child check the answer using addition.

Add up on the open number line to find each difference. Then add to check your work.

1. $994 - 770 =$ _____

_____ + _____ = _____

⟵——————————————⟶

2. $831 - 716 =$ _____

_____ + _____ = _____

⟵——————————————⟶

Solve each problem. Check your work.

3. Reasoning April has 365 stickers. She gives 238 stickers to Gwen. How many stickers does April have left?

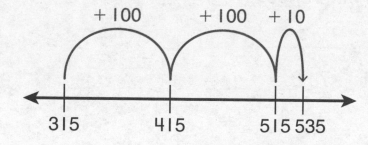

_____ stickers

4. Math and Science A group of birds had 362 seeds. Some seeds fell to the ground. Now the birds have 237 seeds. How many seeds fell?

_____ seeds

5. Higher Order Thinking Ricky added up on the number line and found 535 − 315 = 210. Is his work correct? Explain.

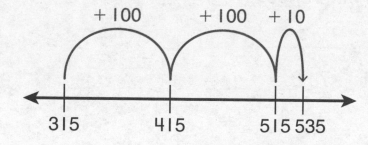

6. ✓Assessment Show one way to add up on the open number line to find 560 − 340. Write the difference. Then explain your work.

560 − 340 = _____

Name _____

Independent Practice ✫ Use any strategy to subtract. Show your work.

5. 598 − 319 = _____

6. 794 − 452 = _____

7. 871 − 355 = _____

8. 649 − 525 = _____

9. 463 − 244 = _____

10. 304 − 198 = _____

11. Number Sense Leo says that the difference of
526 − 217 is greater than 200.
Is what Leo says reasonable? Why or why not?

Sometimes it can help
to use numbers that are close
but easier to subtract.

_____

_____

_____

12. Tia collected cans to raise money for school. She collected 569 cans on Monday. Tia collected some more cans on Tuesday. Now she has 789 cans. How many cans did Tia collect on Tuesday?

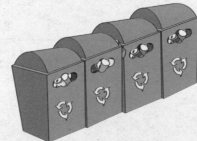

_____ cans

13. **Reasoning** Felipe has 453 stamps in his collection. Emily has 762 stamps in her collection. How many more stamps does Emily have?

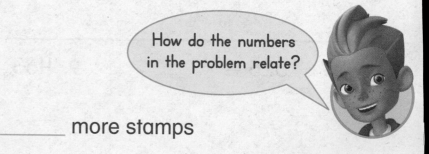

How do the numbers in the problem relate?

_____ more stamps

14. **Higher Order Thinking** Write a subtraction problem about recycling. Use 3-digit numbers. Use pictures, numbers, or words to solve the problem.

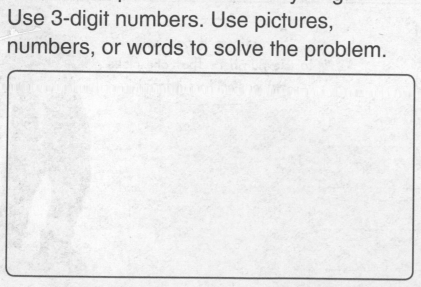

15. ✓**Assessment** On Saturday, 28 fewer boys than girls played in soccer matches. If 214 girls played, how many boys played?

Ⓐ 186

Ⓑ 166

Ⓒ 156

Ⓓ 136

Name _____

 Help   Tools   Games

Another Look! Find 361 − 142.

One Way

Start at 361 and count back 142.

Remember, 142 is
1 hundred, 4 tens, and 2 ones.

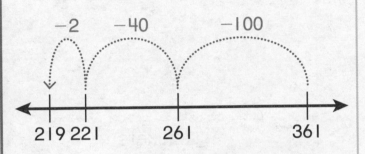

−2   −40   −100

219 221   261   361

So, 361 − 142 = 219.

Another Way

Use easier numbers.

140 is easier to subtract than 142.
142 = 140 + 2

Subtract 140.
Then subtract 2 more.

$$
\begin{array}{r} 361 \\ -140 \\ \hline 221 \end{array}
\qquad
\begin{array}{r} 221 \\ -2 \\ \hline 219 \end{array}
$$

So, 361 − 142 = 219.

HOME ACTIVITY Ask your child to show you how to subtract 431 − 216. Have your child explain every step of the subtraction.

Use any strategy to subtract. Show your work.

1. 412 − 103 = _____

2. 398 − 235 = _____

3. 753 − 304 = _____

Make Sense Mrs. Anderson gives star stickers to her class. She starts with 989 stickers in September. Find out how many she has left as the months go by. Use any strategy. Show your work.

4. In September, Mrs. Anderson gives away 190 stickers.

$989 - 190 =$ _____

_____ stickers

5. In October and November, Mrs. Anderson gives away 586 stickers.

_____ – _____ = _____

_____ stickers

6. In December, Mrs. Anderson gives away 109 more stickers.

_____ – _____ = _____

_____ stickers

7. Higher Order Thinking Kelly cuts out 265 strips of paper for an art project. She glues some strips of paper to her piece of art. Now she has 138 strips of paper left. How many strips of paper did Kelly use?

$265 -$ _____ $= 138$

_____ strips of paper

8. ✅**Assessment** Jimmy's hive has 528 bees. Julie's hive has 204 bees. How many more bees does Jimmy's hive have than Julie's hive?

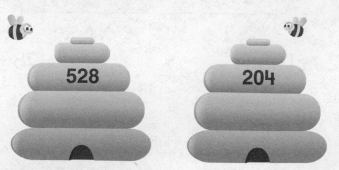

Ⓐ 224

Ⓑ 304

Ⓒ 314

Ⓓ 324

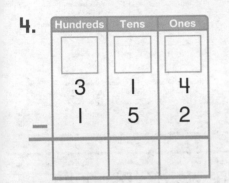

Independent Practice

Subtract. Draw place-value blocks to show your work. Regroup if needed.

4.

Hundreds	Tens	Ones
☐	☐	☐
3	1	4
− 1	5	2

Hundreds	Tens	Ones

5.

Hundreds	Tens	Ones
☐	☐	☐
6	5	3
− 4	1	9

Hundreds	Tens	Ones

6.

Hundreds	Tens	Ones
☐	☐	☐
4	3	8
− 1	6	2

Hundreds	Tens	Ones

7.

Hundreds	Tens	Ones
☐	☐	☐
6	6	2
− 4	8	0

Hundreds	Tens	Ones

8. Higher Order Thinking Find the missing numbers. Explain your steps for solving.

Hundreds	Tens	Ones
☐	☐	☐
8	5	4
− 2	9	
		2

Hundreds	Tens	Ones

_____
_____
_____
_____

9. **Model** Jeff has 517 baseball cards. He has 263 football cards. How many more baseball cards than football cards does he have?

Hundreds	Tens	Ones

Hundreds	Tens	Ones

_____ more baseball cards

10. **Higher Order Thinking** Choose a number between 330 and 336. Subtract 180 from your number. Draw place-value blocks to show the difference.

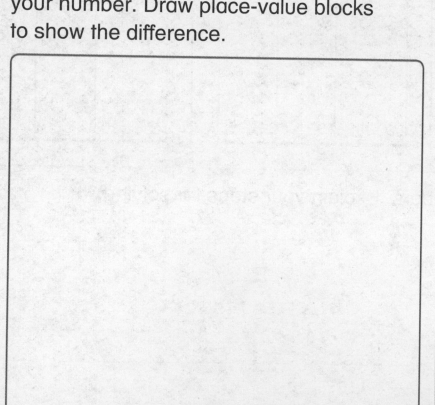

11. ✓**Assessment** There were 342 adults at the movie. There were 526 children at the movie. How many more children than adults were at the movie?

Ⓐ 184

Ⓑ 224

Ⓒ 284

Ⓓ 868

The adults and children were all at the movie at the same time.

Name _____

Another Look! You can follow these steps to subtract three-digit numbers.

Find 327 − 164.

Step 1: Subtract the ones. Regroup if needed.

Step 2: Subtract the tens. Regroup if needed.

Step 3: Subtract the hundreds.

HOME ACTIVITY Have your child draw place-value blocks to model and find 583 − 274.

Think: Regroup 1 hundred for 10 tens. Draw place-value blocks to help.

Hundreds	Tens	Ones
2	12	
3	2	7
− 1	6	4
1	6	3

Hundreds	Tens	Ones

327 − 164 = __163__

Subtract to find each difference. Draw place-value blocks to help.

1.

Hundreds	Tens	Ones
4	14	
5	4	9
− 2	9	5
2	5	4

Hundreds	Tens	Ones

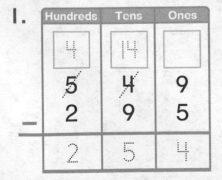

2.

Hundreds	Tens	Ones
8	3	5
− 5	1	6

Hundreds	Tens	Ones

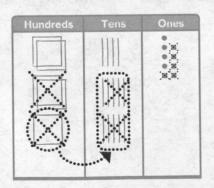

Solve the problems below. Remember to regroup when you need to.

3. **Generalize** Subtract. Then circle the problems where you regrouped to solve.

Hundreds	Tens	Ones
4	3	7
− 1	6	4

Hundreds	Tens	Ones
5	7	8
− 2	6	4

Hundreds	Tens	Ones
3	8	1
− 1	9	0

Hundreds	Tens	Ones
9	8	9
− 3	6	2

Hundreds	Tens	Ones
6	2	3
− 3	7	1

4. **Higher Order Thinking** Look at the differences in the problems above. Find two that you can use to subtract and get a difference of 354. Then complete the workmat to show your subtraction.

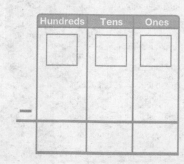

5. ✓**Assessment** A farm has 319 animals. 136 of the animals are pigs. How many animals are **NOT** pigs?

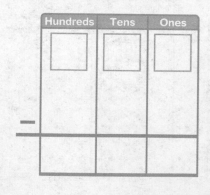

Hundreds	Tens	Ones

_____ animals are **NOT** pigs.

6. ✓**Assessment** An office building is 332 feet tall. An apartment building is 208 feet tall. How many feet taller is the office building?

Ⓐ 124

Ⓑ 134

Ⓒ 136

Ⓓ 540

Solve

Solve & Share

Find 532 − 215. Use any strategy. Then explain why your strategy works.

Lesson 11-6

Explain Subtraction Strategies

I can ...
explain why subtraction strategies work using models, place value, and mental math.

I can also reason about math.

Find 437 − 245. Use any strategy.

One way Draw place-value blocks to show 437. Regroup 1 hundred as 10 tens. Then subtract.

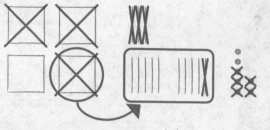

So, 437 − 245 = ___192___.

Another way is to use an open number line to subtract.

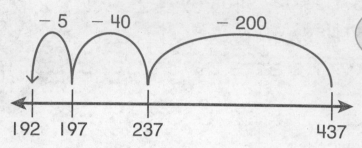

So, 437 − 245 = ___192___.

You can count back the hundreds, then the tens, and then the ones.

Do You Understand?

Show Me! Do you think both of these strategies are good for finding 437 − 245? Explain.

☆ **Guided Practice** ☆ Subtract any way you choose. Show your work. Then explain why the strategy works.

1. 345 − 116 = _229_

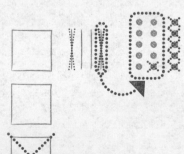

Tools   Assessment

Independent Practice

Choose any strategy to solve each subtraction problem. Show your work. Then explain why the stategy works.

2. $312 - 179 =$ _____

_____

_____

_____

3. $464 - 155 =$ _____

_____

_____

_____

4. $612 - 478 =$ _____

_____

_____

_____

5. Number Sense Use place value to find $748 - 319$. Complete the equations.

$$319 = 300 + \underline{\quad} + 9$$

Hundreds: $748 - \underline{\quad} = \underline{\quad}$

Tens: $\underline{\quad} - 10 = \underline{\quad}$

Ones: $\underline{\quad} - \underline{\quad} = \underline{\quad}$

6. **Explain** Ava wants to use mental math to find 352 − 149. Show how she could find the difference. Is this a good strategy for Eva to use? Explain why or why not.

7. **Higher Order Thinking** Kristin found 562 − 399 = 163 using an open number line. She added up to subtract. First she added 1, then 100, and then 62.

   Draw Kristin's number line. Do you think Kristin's strategy was helpful? Explain.

8. ✓**Assessment** Jeff counted back on this open number line to find 812 − 125.

   Use the numbers on the cards to find the missing numbers in the open number line. Write the missing numbers.

   | 702 | 812 | 687 | 712 |

   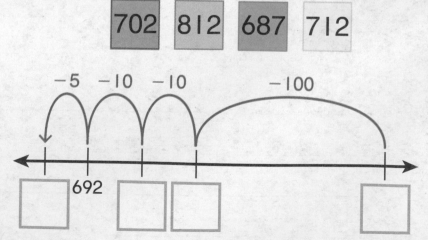

Name _____

Help Tools Games

Explain Subtraction Strategies

Another Look! Find 725 − 592.

One Way Add up to subtract.

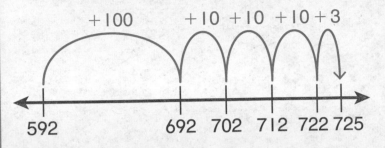

Add hundreds, tens, and ones.

$100 + 10 + 10 + 10 + 3 = 133$

So, $725 − 592 = 133$.

Another Way It is easy to subtract 725 − 600 mentally. So, add 8 to 592 to make 600.

$$\begin{array}{r} 725 \\ -\ 600 \\ \hline 125 \end{array} \qquad \begin{array}{r} 1 \\ 125 \\ +\ \ 8 \\ \hline 133 \end{array}$$

Since you added 8 to 592, you need to add 8 to 125 to get the difference.

So, $725 − 592 = 133$.

HOME ACTIVITY Ask your child to find 597 − 217 using a subtraction strategy he or she chooses. Then have your child explain why he or she thinks the strategy works.

Choose any strategy to solve each subtraction problem. Show your work. Then explain why the strategy works.

1. $926 − 407 = $ _____

2. $532 − 241 = $ _____

_____

_____

Solve each problem.

3. **Explain** Tanner wants to count back on an open number line to find 577 − 479. Marci wants to use mental math to find the difference. Which strategy do you think works better? Why? Show how you would find 577 − 479.

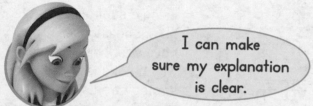

I can make sure my explanation is clear.

4. **Higher Order Thinking** Danny wants to draw place-value blocks to find 342 − 127. Draw the blocks he would use. Explain why this strategy works.

_____

_____

_____

5. ✅**Assessment** Landon counted back on this open number line to find 898 − 133.

Use the numbers on the cards to find the missing numbers in the open number line. Write the missing numbers.

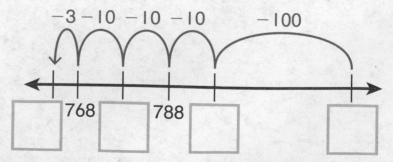

768   788

Name _____

Solve & Share

Jody wants to bake 350 muffins.
She bakes one batch of 160 muffins and one batch
of 145 muffins. How many more muffins does Jody
need to bake?

Solve any way you choose. Show your work.

I can ...
solve problems that take more
than one step.

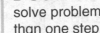
I can also add and
subtract three-digit numbers.

Thinking Habits

What do I know?

What do I need to find?

How can I check that
my solution makes
sense?

Grade 2 wants to sell 10 more tickets to the school play than Grade 1.

Grade 1 sold 476 tickets. Grade 2 sold 439 tickets.

How many more tickets does Grade 2 have to sell to reach their goal?

How can I make sense of the problem?

I can see what I know. I can find hidden questions. I can choose a strategy to solve the problem.

An easy first step is to answer the hidden question.

What is the Grade 2 goal?

Grade 2 Goal

476 + 10 = 486 tickets

Now I can subtract the number of tickets Grade 2 sold from their goal.

$$\begin{array}{r} 7\,16 \\ 4\,8\,6 \\ -4\,3\,9 \\ \hline 4\,7 \end{array}$$

Grade 2 needs to sell 47 more tickets to reach their goal.

Do You Understand?

Show Me! What questions can you ask yourself when you get stuck? Be ready to explain how questions can help.

☆ Guided Practice

Solve the problem. Remember to ask yourself questions to help. Show your work.

1. Kim had 455 shells. First, she gives 134 of the shells to a friend. Then she finds 54 more shells. How many shells does Kim have now?

What will you find first? Which operation will you use?

Independent Practice ☆   Use the table to solve each problem. Show your work.

Weights of Wild Animals (in pounds)				
Animal	Arctic Wolf	Black Bear	Grizzly Bear	Mule Deer	Polar Bear
Weight	176	270	990	198	945

2. How much heavier is a grizzly bear than an arctic wolf and a black bear together?

3. How much less does a black bear weigh than the weight of 2 mule deer?

4. How much more does a polar bear weigh than an arctic wolf, a black bear, and a mule deer together?

You know how to add three 2-digit numbers.

How can that help you add three 3-digit numbers?

✓ **Performance Assessment**

Big Truck

The picture at the right shows the height of a truck and the height of a smokestack on top of the truck. The height of a bridge is 144 inches.

Use the information at the right.
Can the truck travel under the bridge?

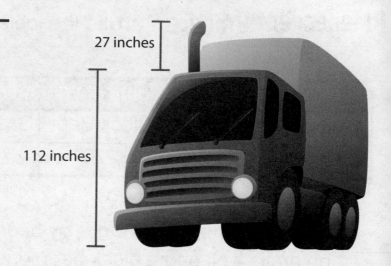

27 inches

112 inches

5. **Make Sense** What do you know? What are you trying to find?

_____

_____

_____

_____

6. **Make Sense** What hidden question do you need to answer first? Find the answer to the hidden question.

7. **Explain** Can the truck travel under the bridge? Show your work. Why does your solution make sense?

Name _____

Another Look! You need to use more than one step to solve some problems.

Read the problem. Complete the steps to solve.

Carl has 254 baseball cards.
He gives 145 cards to John and 56 to Amy.
How many cards does Carl have left?

Step 1 Add to find the number of cards Carl gives to John and Amy.

$$145 + 56 = 201$$

Step 2 Subtract the number of cards Carl gives away from the number of cards he has.

$$254 - 201 = 53 \qquad \underline{53} \text{ cards left}$$

Think: Is there a hidden question to answer first?

Think: Does my answer make sense?

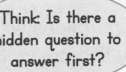

Solve the problem. Show your work.
Be ready to explain why your answer makes sense.

1. Mr. Wu buys a box of 300 nails. He uses 156 nails to build a deck. He uses 98 nails to build stairs. How many nails are left?

A School of Fish

Some fish travel in large groups called schools. Swimming in schools helps keep fish safe.

375 fish are swimming in a school. First, 47 fish swim away. Then 116 more fish join the school. How many fish are in the school now?

2. **Reasoning** Which operations will you use to find how many fish are in the school now? Explain.

_____

_____

_____

3. **Generalize** Are there now more or less than 375 fish in the school? Explain how you know.

_____

_____

_____

4. **Make Sense** How many fish are in the school now? Show your work.

Color a path from **Start** to **Finish**. Follow the sums and differences that are even numbers. You can only move up, down, right, or left.

TOPIC 11

Fluency Practice Activity

I can ...
add and subtract within 20.

Start								
6 + 6	10 + 8	16 − 8	9 − 0	14 − 4	6 − 2	10 + 10	8 − 3	2 + 7
5 + 4	9 − 4	11 − 9	10 + 5	13 − 5	2 − 1	7 + 9	10 − 9	10 + 9
15 − 8	3 + 10	5 + 1	9 + 8	6 + 8	12 − 5	7 + 7	16 − 9	13 − 8
12 − 9	14 − 7	14 − 6	16 − 7	9 + 9	5 + 6	8 − 6	2 + 5	4 + 7
8 + 9	9 + 6	7 + 5	12 − 8	1 + 7	18 − 9	6 − 0	17 − 9	15 − 7

Finish

A-Z Glossary

Word List
- bar diagram
- difference
- hundreds
- mental math
- open number line
- regroup

Understand Vocabulary

Draw a line from each term to its example.

1. hundreds

2. bar diagram

3. regroup

$63 = 5$ tens and 13 ones

<u>8</u>23

---

4. This open number line is incomplete. It needs to show counting back to find $538 - 115$. Write in the missing numbers and labels.

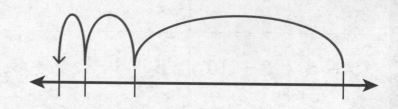

Use Vocabulary in Writing

5. Find $205 - 121$. Use terms from the Word List to explain your work.

$$205$$
$$-121$$

Name _____

Set A _____

You can subtract 10 or 100 mentally.

$549 - 10 = ?$
The tens digit goes down by 1.
$549 - 10 = 539$

$549 - 100 = ?$
The hundreds digit goes down by 1.
$549 - 100 = 449$

Subtract using mental math.

1. $426 - 10 = $ _____

   $426 - 100 = $ _____

2. $287 - 10 = $ _____

   $287 - 100 = $ _____

3. $800 - 10 = $ _____

   $800 - 100 = $ _____

Set B _____

Find $673 - 458$. Start at 458 on an open number line. Add up to 673.

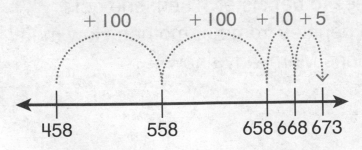

Add $100 + 100 + 10 + 5 = 215$

So, $673 - 458 = \underline{215}$.

Use an open number line to subtract.

4. $449 - 217 = $ _____

5. $903 - 678 = $ _____

You can draw place-value blocks to show subtraction. Find 327 − 219.

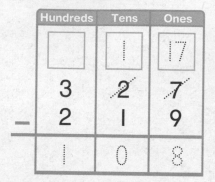
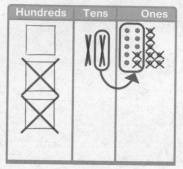

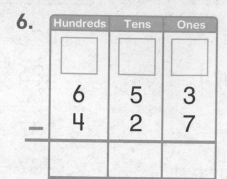

Hundreds	Tens	Ones
	1	17
3	2̷	7̷
− 2	1	9
1	0	8

Subtract. Draw models and regroup if needed.

6.

Hundreds	Tens	Ones
6	5	3
− 4	2	7

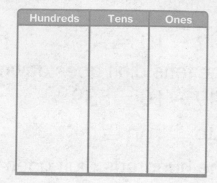

Hundreds	Tens	Ones

Thinking Habits

Persevere

What do I know?

What do I need to find?

How can I check that my solution makes sense?

Solve the problem.
Ask yourself questions to help.

7. Marni has 354 pennies. First, she gives 149 pennies to her sister. Then, she gets 210 more pennies from her mother. How many pennies does Marni have now?

1. Which equals 100 less than 763?
Choose all that apply.

☐ 663

☐ 600 + 60 + 3

☐ 863

☐ 800 + 60 + 3

2. The open number line below shows subtraction.

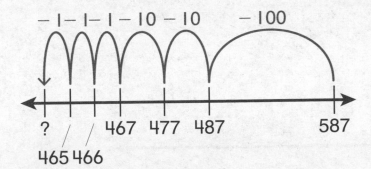

Complete the equation. Write the numbers being subtracted and the difference.

_____ − _____ = _____

3. Is the difference equal to 462? Choose Yes or No. Use different strategies to subtract.

998 − 536 = ?   ○ Yes ○ No

842 − 380 = ?   ○ Yes ○ No

687 − 125 = ?   ○ Yes ○ No

924 − 462 = ?   ○ Yes ○ No

4. There are 537 boys and 438 girls at the concert. How many more boys than girls are at the concert?

Ⓐ 89

Ⓑ 99

Ⓒ 101

Ⓓ 109

5. Show how to add up on an open number line to find 740 − 490. Then write the difference below.

740 − 490 = _____

6. Look at your work in Item 5. Why can you use adding up on an open number line to find 740 − 490? Choose all that apply.

☐ You can always add up to subtract on an open number line.

☐ You can't always add up to subtract on an open number line.

☐ An open number line helps you break apart numbers to subtract.

☐ An open number line should be used for any type of problem.

7. Use the numbers on the cards to find the missing numbers in the subtraction problem. Use the place-value models to help. Write the missing numbers.

| 7 | 6 | 1 | 2 |

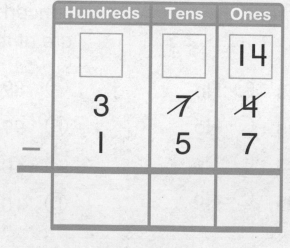

Hundreds	Tens	Ones
☐	☐	14
3	7̸	4̸
− 1	5	7

Hundreds	Tens	Ones
☐	‖	••••
☐	‖‖‖	
☐		

Name _____

Performance Assessment

Bead It!

The chart shows the number of beads sold at Betty's craft store for 4 weeks.

Number of Beads Sold	
Week 1	400
Week 2	536
Week 3	675
Week 4	289

1. How many more beads did Betty sell in Week 2 than in Week 1? Use mental math to solve. Write the missing numbers in the equation.

_____ – _____ = _____

_____ more beads

2. 458 glass beads were sold in Week 3. The other beads sold in Week 3 were plastic. How many plastic beads were sold in Week 3?

Use the open number line to solve.

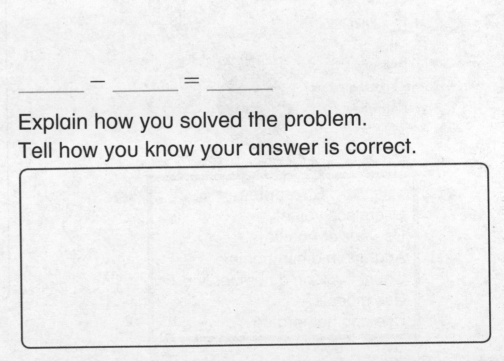

_____ – _____ = _____

Explain how you solved the problem. Tell how you know your answer is correct.

3. Dex buys 243 beads at Betty's store. He uses 118 of them to make a bracelet. How many beads does Dex have left?

Solve the problem. Show your work. Explain which strategy you used.

_____ − _____ = _____

_____ beads

Here are some strategies you can use.

Strategies
Use place value.
Use easier numbers.
Add up on a number line.
Count back on a number line.
Use models.
Use another strategy.

4. Ginny buys 958 beads. 245 beads are blue. 309 beads are orange. 153 beads are white. The rest are red. How many red beads does Ginny buy?

Part A
What is the hidden question in the problem?

_____

_____

Part B
Solve the problem. Show your work. Explain which strategy you used.

_____ red beads

Topic 11 | Performance Assessment

Measuring Length

Essential Question: What are ways to measure length?

Digital Resources

Solve Learn Glossary

Tools Assessment Help Games

Look how tall sunflowers grow!

Sunlight and water help plants grow.

Wow! Let's do this project and learn more.

Math and Science Project: Growing and Measuring

Find Out Grow bean plants. Give them numbers. Put some in sunlight. Put some in a dark place. Water some of the plants. Do not water some of the plants. See how the plants in each group grow.

Journal: Make a Book Show what you learn in a book. In your book, also:

• Tell if plants need sunlight and water to grow.

• Find plants to measure. Draw pictures of the plants. Tell how tall each plant is.

Name _____

Review What You Know

A-Z Vocabulary

1. Draw a line to show the **length** of the bat.

2. School is getting out. Circle **a.m.** or **p.m.**

a.m.

p.m.

3. Draw clock hands to show **quarter past** 10.

Estimating and Measuring Length

4. Use snap cubes.

Estimate the length.

about _____ cubes

Measure the length.

about _____ cubes

5.

Estimate the length.

about _____ cubes

Measure the length.

about _____ cubes

Skip Counting

6. Write the missing numbers.

5, 10, _____, 20, _____

210, 220, _____, 240

400, _____, 600, 700

Look for a pattern.

688 six hundred eighty-eight

Topic 12

My Word Cards

Study the words on the front of the card.
Complete the activity on the back.

A-Z
Glossary

estimate

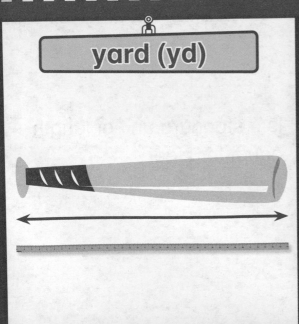

I think the book is about 1 foot long.

inch (in.)

0   1   2
INCHES

foot (ft)

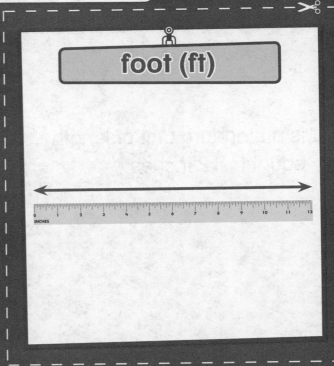

0 1 2 3 4 5 6 7 8 9 10 11 12
INCHES

yard (yd)

length

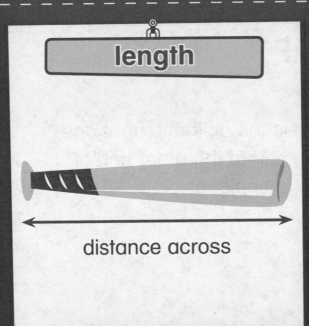

distance across

height

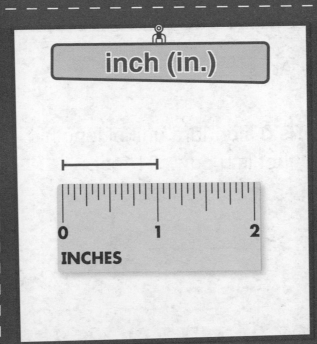

My Word Cards

Use what you know to complete the sentences.
Extend learning by writing your own sentence using each word.

A ____________________

is a standard unit of length equal to 12 inches.

An ____________________

is a standard unit of length that is a part of 1 foot.

When you

____________________,

you make a good guess.

____

is how tall an object is from bottom to top.

____

is the distance from one end to the other end of an object.

A ____________________

is a standard unit of length equal to 3 feet.

My Word Cards

Study the words on the front of the card.
Complete the activity on the back.

A-Z
Glossary

nearest inch

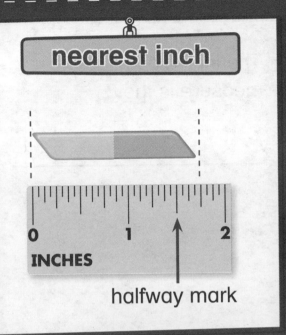

INCHES

halfway mark

centimeter (cm)

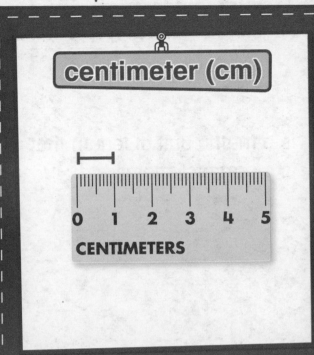

CENTIMETERS

meter (m)

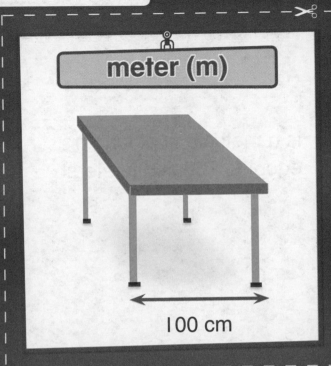

100 cm

nearest centimeter

CENTIMETERS

halfway mark

My Word Cards

Use what you know to complete the sentences.
Extend learning by writing your own sentence using each word.

A _____

is a metric unit of length
equal to 100 centimeters.

A _____

is a metric unit of length that
is a part of 1 meter.

The inch closest to the
measure is the

_____.

The closest centimeter
to the measure is the

_____.

Name _____

Solve & Share

Your thumb is about 1 inch long. Use your thumb to find three objects that are each about 1 inch long. Draw the objects.

From your elbow to your fingers is about 1 foot long. Use this part of your arm to find three objects that are each about 1 foot long. Draw the objects.

I can ...
estimate the length of an object by relating the length of the object to a measurement I know.

I can also be precise in my work.

about 1 inch	about 1 foot

You can use the length of objects you know to **estimate** the length of other objects.

Some small paper clips are 1 inch (1 in.) long.

Use a small paperclip to estimate how long the eraser is.

The eraser is about 2 paper clips long. So, it is about 2 inches long.

You can estimate with objects that are about 1 foot (ft) and 1 yard (yd) in length, too.

Do You Understand?

Show Me! Is your height closer to 4 feet or 4 yards? How do you know?

☆ Guided Practice ☆

Write the name and length of an object whose length you know. Then use that object to help you estimate the length of the object shown.

Object	Object Whose Length I Know	Estimate
1.	My paper clip is <u>1 inch</u> long.	My pencil is about _____ long.
2.	My <u>book</u> is _____ long.	My desk is about _____ long.

Topic 12 | Lesson 1

Independent Practice

Write the name and length of an object whose length you know.
Then use that object to help you estimate the length of the object shown.

Object	Object Whose Length I Know	Estimate
3.	My _____ is _____ long.	My hand is about _____ long.
4.	My _____ is _____ long.	My chair is about _____ high.

5. **Higher Order Thinking** Would you estimate the distance from your classroom to the principal's office in inches, feet or yards? Explain.

_____

_____

_____

A giant step is about a yard.

_____

6. **A-Z Vocabulary** Complete the sentence using one of the words below.

exact   **estimated**   **inch**

An _____ measurement is a good guess.

7. **Reasoning** Joy and Kyle estimate the height of their classroom. Joy estimates the height to be 10 feet. Kyle estimates the height to be 10 yards. Who has the better estimate? Explain.

_____

_____

_____

_____

8. **Higher Order Thinking** A city wants to build a bridge over a river. Should they plan out an exact length of the bridge or is an estimated length good enough? Explain.

_____

_____

_____

9. **✓Assessment** Draw a line from each estimate to a matching object.

| About 1 inch | About 1 foot | About 3 feet |

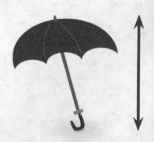

Name _____

Another Look!

A small paper clip is about 1 inch long.

about 1 inch

A scarf is about 1 yard long. There are 3 feet in 1 yard.

about 1 yard

A tablet computer is about 1 foot long. There are 12 inches in 1 foot.

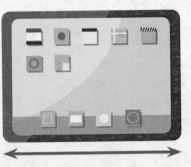

about 1 foot

HOME ACTIVITY Have your child identify three objects that are about 1 inch, 1 foot, and 1 yard in length or height.

About how long or tall is each object? Circle the answer.

1.
about 1 inch

about 1 foot

about 1 yard

2.
about 1 inch

about 1 foot

about 1 yard

3.
about 1 inch

about 1 foot

about 1 yard

Reasoning Choose three objects and estimate their length or height in inches, feet, or yards. Draw a picture and write the name of each object. Write the estimated length or height next to each object.

4.

5.

6.

7. **Higher Order Thinking** Mia has 4 tiles. Jake has 5 tiles. Each tile is about 1 inch long. They use all of their tiles to measure the height of this water bottle. What is the height of the water bottle?

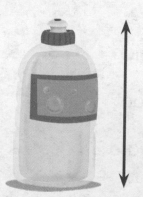

About _____ inches

8. ✅**Assessment** Draw a line from each estimate to a matching object.

About 1 inch	About 1 foot	About 3 feet

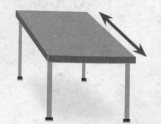 

Name _____

Independent Practice

Estimate the height or length of each object.
Then use a ruler to measure.

3.

length of a
book bag

Estimate	Measure
about _____ inches	about _____ inches
about _____ inches	about _____ inches

4.

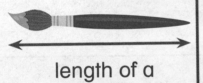

length of a
paintbrush

5.

height of
a cup

Estimate	Measure
about _____ inches	about _____ inches
about _____ inches	about _____ inches

6.

length of a
crayon box

Higher Order Thinking Think about how to use a ruler to solve each problem.

7. Jason measures an object. The object is just shorter than the halfway mark between 8 and 9 on his inch ruler. How long is the object?

about _____ inches

8. Gina measures an object. The object is just longer than the halfway mark between 9 and 10 on her inch ruler. How long is the object?

about _____ inches

9. **Explain** Pam says that each cherry is about 1 inch wide. Is she correct? Explain.

_____

_____

_____

10. **A-Z Vocabulary** Find an object in the classroom that measures about 6 inches. Write a sentence to describe the object. Use these words.

estimate   inches

_____

_____

_____

11. **Higher Order Thinking** Explain how to use an inch ruler to measure the length of an object.

_____

_____

_____

12. **✓ Assessment** Use a ruler. About how many inches long are the two stamps together?

Ⓐ 4 inches   Ⓒ 2 inches

Ⓑ 3 inches   Ⓓ 1 inch

Name _____

Another Look! You can use a ruler to measure inches.

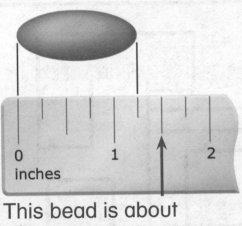

0 inches   1   2

This bead is about

__1__ inch long.

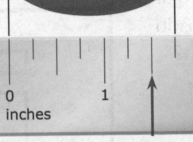

0 inches   1   2

This bead is about

__2__ inches long.

Remember to use the 0 line of the ruler to start.

To measure to the nearest inch, compare the length to the halfway mark between inches.

HOME ACTIVITY Ask your child to find items at home that are about 1 inch, about 6 inches, and about 12 inches long.

Estimate the height or length. Then use a ruler to measure.

1. height of a book

My Favorite Book

Estimate	Measure
about ____ inches	about ____ inches
about ____ inches	about ____ inches

2. length of a pencil

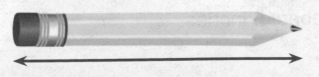

3. **Number Sense** Estimate how long the path is to get out of this maze.

about _____ inches

4. **Make Sense** Draw a path from the start to the exit. Use a ruler to measure each part of your path. Add the lengths together. About how long is the path?

about _____ inches

Start

Exit

5. How close to the answer was your estimate?

_____

6. **Higher Order Thinking** Gina says this straw is about 2 inches long. Sal says it is about 3 inches long. Who is correct? Explain.

_____

_____

7. ✅**Assessment** Use a ruler. Measure the length of the pencil in inches. Which is the correct measurement?

Ⓐ about 2 inches

Ⓑ about 3 inches

Ⓒ about 4 inches

Ⓓ about 5 inches

Name _____

Independent Practice Estimate the length of each object. Choose a ruler, yardstick, or measuring tape to measure. Write the tool you used.

	Estimate	Measure	Tool
4. 	about ____ inches	about ____ inches	_____
5. 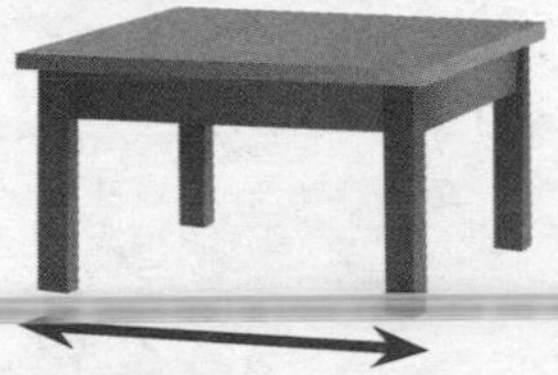	about ____ feet	about ____ feet	_____
6. 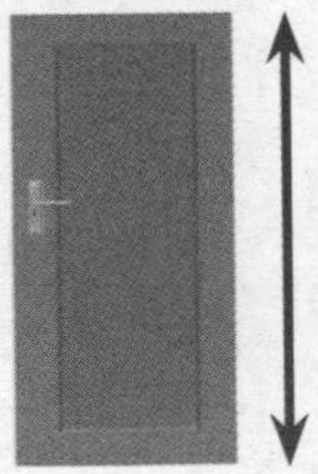	about ____ yards	about ____ yards	_____

7. **Higher Order Thinking** Explain how you could use a foot ruler to measure the length of a room in feet.

_____

_____

_____

Problem Solving ☆ Solve each problem.

8. Generalize Circle the real object that is about 4 feet in length.

9. Number Sense Explain how to use a yardstick to measure the length of an object.

_____
_____
_____
_____
_____
_____
_____

10. Higher Order Thinking Find an object in the classroom that you estimate measures about 2 feet. Draw the object.

What tool would you use to measure it? Explain why you chose the tool you did.

_____

11. ✓**Assessment** Jon sets two of the same real objects next to each other. Together, they have a length of about 4 feet. Which is the object Jon uses?

Ⓐ

Ⓒ

Ⓑ

Ⓓ

Topic 12 | Lesson 3

Name _____

Another Look! You can use a yardstick to measure objects to the nearest foot.

Remember, I foot is 12 inches long.
So 2 feet are 24 inches long.
I yard is 36 inches long
or 3 feet long.

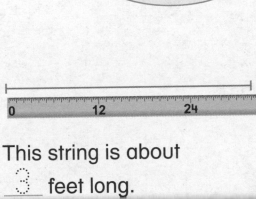

Think: Is the string closer to 2 feet long or closer to 3 feet long?

HOME ACTIVITY Have your child identify three objects at home that are about I inch, I foot, and I yard in length.

This string is about
__2__ feet long.

This string is about
__3__ feet long.

 Estimate the height or length of each object. Then measure.

I. the height of the doorway

Estimate: about _____ feet

Measure: about _____ feet

2. the height of a chair

Estimate: about _____ feet

Measure: about _____ feet

3. the width of a window

Estimate: about _____ feet

Measure: about _____ feet

4. Reasoning Draw a picture of and name objects that have these lengths.

more than 6 inches but less than 1 foot

more than 1 foot but less than 2 feet

more than 2 feet but less than 1 yard

5. Math and Science Jay planted sunflowers in a sunny spot. He gave them water and watched them grow to be taller than he is. He measured the heights of the plants when they were full-grown. Were they 8 inches or 8 feet tall? Explain.

_____

_____

_____

_____

6. Higher Order Thinking Which tool would you choose to measure the number of inches around your waist? Explain.

_____

_____

_____

_____

7. ✓Assessment Use a ruler. About how long is the crayon?

Ⓐ about 1 inch

Ⓑ about 2 inches

Ⓒ about 4 inches

Ⓓ about 6 inches

Name _____

Solve & Share

Choose an object. Measure your object in feet. Then measure it in inches.

Do you need more feet or more inches to measure your object? Why?

I can ...
estimate and measure the length and height of objects in inches, feet, and yards.

I can also use math tools correctly.

about ____ feet long

about ____ inches long

more feet   more inches

You can use different units to measure objects.
Which would you use more of to measure the length of the bookcase, feet or yards?

Measure the bookcase in feet.

It is about 3 feet long.

1   2   3

Measure the bookcase in yards.

It is about 1 yard long.

1

I used more feet than yards because a foot is a smaller unit than a yard.

Do You Understand?

Show Me! Would you use a ruler, a yardstick, or measuring tape to measure the height of a door? Why?

☆ **Guided Practice** ☆   Measure each object using different units. Circle the unit you use more of to measure each object.

1.

about _____ feet   about _____ yards

more feet

more yards

2.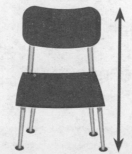

about _____ inches   about _____ feet

more inches

more feet

Topic 12 | Lesson 4

Name _____

Help Tools Games

Another Look! You can measure using different units.

Derrick measured the gift box in inches and in feet.

The gift box is about

_____ inches long.

The gift box is about

_____ foot long.

It takes more inches than feet to measure the gift box because an inch is a smaller unit.

If you use smaller units, you need to use more units.

HOME ACTIVITY Have your child use a foot ruler to measure objects in both inches and in feet. Then ask your child if he or she used more inches or more feet to measure each object.

Measure each object using different units.
Circle the unit you need more of to measure each object.

1.

about _____ feet   about _____ yards

more feet

more yards

2.

about _____ inches   about _____ feet

more inches

more feet

Topic 12 | Lesson 4

Digital Resources at SavvasRealize.com

seven hundred fifteen **715**

3. Explain Trina says that her dollhouse is about 8 yards tall. Is Trina's estimate a good estimate? Explain.

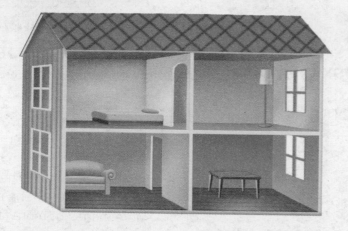

_____

_____

_____

4. Higher Order Thinking Sarah wants to measure the length of her math book. Should she use inches, feet, or yards? Explain.

_____

_____

_____

5. ✓**Assessment** Which unit would you need the most of to measure the height of the umbrella?

Ⓐ inches

Ⓑ feet

Ⓒ yards

Ⓓ all the same

6. ✓**Assessment** Which is the best estimate for the length of a pen?

Ⓐ about 10 inches

Ⓑ about 6 inches

Ⓒ about 5 feet

Ⓓ about 10 yards

Name _____

Another Look! You can use a ruler to measure centimeters.

To measure to the nearest centimeter, look at the halfway mark between centimeters. If the object is longer, use the greater number. If the object is shorter, use the smaller number.

HOME ACTIVITY Ask your child to find items at home that measure about 1 centimeter, about 10 centimeters, and about 100 centimeters. If possible, use a ruler to measure each object.

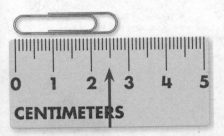

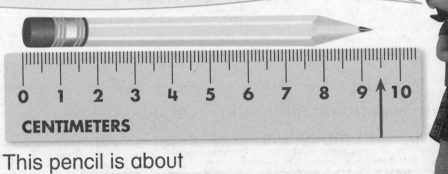

The paper clip is about __3__ centimeters long.

This pencil is about __9__ centimeters long.

Estimate the height or length. Then use a ruler to measure.

1. length of a tape dispenser

Estimate	Measure
about ____ centimeters	about ____ centimeters
about ____ centimeters	about ____ centimeters

2. height of a book

3. **Use Tools** Measure the length of this spoon in centimeters. About how long is the spoon?

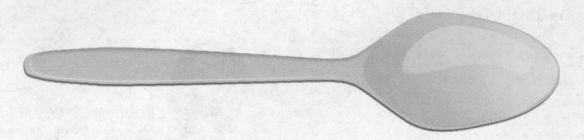

About _____ centimeters   What tool did you use? _____

4. **Higher Order Thinking** Mia has a string that is shown below. Circle the shapes that Mia can make with part of her string.

Use the measurements given on the shapes to decide.

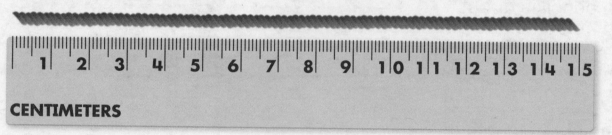

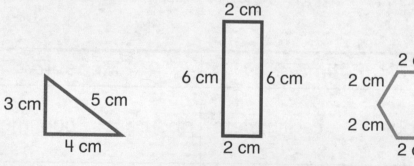

5. ✅**Assessment** Measure this paper clip. How many centimeters long is the paper clip?

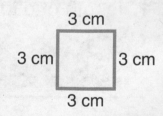

_____ centimeters

Topic 12 | Lesson 5

Name _____

Solve & Share

Which objects in the classroom are about 3 centimeters long?
Which objects are about 1 meter long?
Show these objects below.

I can ...
estimate measures and use a ruler, meter stick, or tape measure to measure length and height to the nearest centimeter or meter.

I can also use math tools correctly.

about 3 centimeters

about 1 meter

You can use a ruler or a meter stick to measure length.

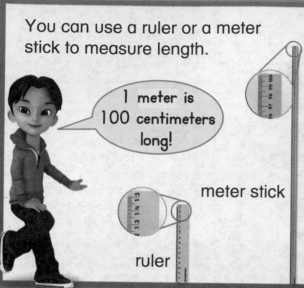

1 meter is 100 centimeters long!

meter stick

ruler

The button is about 1 centimeter (cm) long.

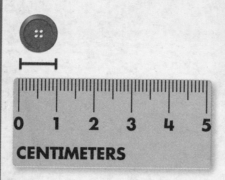

CENTIMETERS

This table is about 1 meter (m) long.

You can also use a measuring tape to measure centimeters and meters.

Do You Understand?

Show Me! Would you measure the length of a house in centimeters or meters? Why?

☆ **Guided Practice** ☆ Match each object with a reasonable estimate of its length.

1.

about 1 cm

2.

about 10 cm

3.

about 1 m

4.

about 10 m

Think about which tool you would use to measure each object.

Topic 12 | Lesson 6

Tools   Assessment

Independent Practice

Estimate the length or height of each real object shown. Then choose a tool and measure. Write the tool you used.

	Estimate	Measure	Tool
5.	about _____ cm	about _____ cm	_____
6.	about _____ m	about _____ m	_____
7.	about _____ cm	about _____ cm	_____
8.	about _____ m	about _____ m	_____

9. Tom uses a meter stick to measure the length of a fence. He moves the meter stick 5 times to measure from one end to the other end. How long is the fence?

_____ meters

10. **Higher Order Thinking** Debbie says that her doll is about 30 meters long. Do you think this is a good estimate? Why or why not?

_____

_____

11. **Be Precise** Choose an object to measure. Use metric units. Draw the object and write your measurements.

Remember to include the units.

12. Circle the real object that would be about 2 meters long.

13. **Higher Order Thinking** Each side of a place-value cube is 1 centimeter long. Use a place value cube to draw a 5 centimeter ruler.

14. ✓**Assessment** Measure each line. Which lines are at least 6 centimeters long? Choose all that apply.

☐

☐

☐ _____

☐ _____

Name _____

Another Look! You can use a meter stick to measure length in meters.

Step 1: Line up a meter stick with one end of an object.

Step 2: Mark the spot where the other end of the meter stick sits on the object.

Step 3: Then move the meter stick so the 0 end starts where you marked.

HOME ACTIVITY Have your child show you an object at home that is about a centimeter long and another object that is about a meter long.

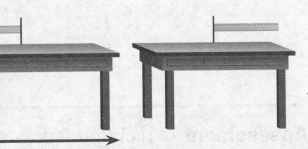

You can measure to the nearest unit.

The table is about __2__ meters long.

Estimate the height or length of each object. Then measure.

1. the length of a table

Estimate:

about _____ meters

Measure:

about _____ meters

2. the height of a chair

Estimate:

about _____ meters

Measure:

about _____ meters

3. the length of your room

Estimate:

about _____ meters

Measure:

about _____ meters

4. Math and Science Sarah put bean plants by a window with sunlight. She watered them every other day. Sarah measured the height of the plants after 3 weeks. Do you think they measured 12 centimeters or 12 meters? Explain.

_____

_____

_____

5. Reasoning What would be a reasonable estimate for the length of a calculator?

about _____ centimeters

6. Higher Order Thinking Do you need fewer centimeters or fewer meters to measure the height of a doorway? Explain.

_____

_____

_____

_____

7. ✓Assessment Which measures are reasonable estimates for the length of a bedroom? Choose all that apply.

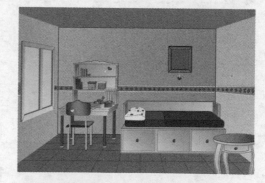

☐ 4 centimeters   ☐ 3 meters

☐ 4 meters   ☐ 30 centimeters

Name _____

Solve & Share

Measure this pencil in inches. Then measure it again in centimeters. Which measurement has more units?

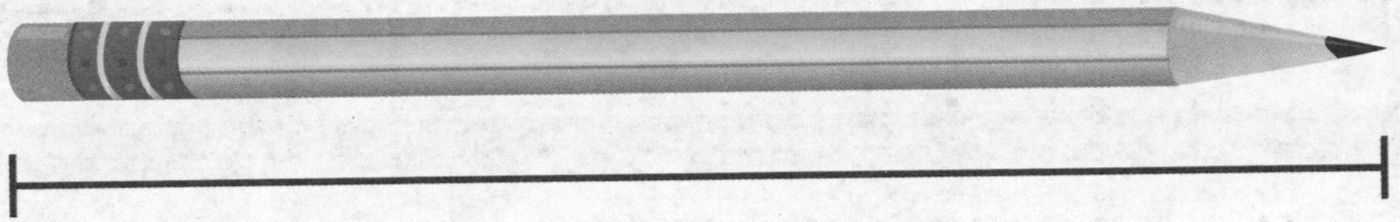

I can ...
measure the length and height of objects using different metric units.

I can also use math tools correctly.

about _____ inches   about _____ centimeters

Which has more units? _____

You can use different units to measure the lengths of objects. Would you use more centimeters or more meters to measure the desk?

Measure the length using centimeters.

It is about 91 centimeters long!

Measure the length using meters.

It is about 1 meter long!

I used more centimeters than meters because a centimeter is a much smaller unit than a meter.

Do You Understand?

Show Me! Would it take more centimeters or more meters to measure the height of a wall? Why?

☆ Guided Practice ☆

Measure each object using different units. Circle the unit you need more of to measure each object.

1.

about _____ centimeters   more centimeters

about _____ meters   more meters

2.

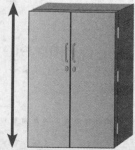

about _____ centimeters   more centimeters

about _____ meters   more meters

Topic 12 | Lesson 7

Name _____

Another Look! You can measure using different units.

Andy measures the length of the television using both centimeters and meters.

The television is about

__1__ meter long.

The television is about

__88__ centimeters long.

It takes fewer meters than centimeters to measure the television.
If you use larger units, you will use fewer of them.

HOME ACTIVITY Select two objects in your home, such as a table or a window. Ask your child if he or she would use more centimeters or meters to measure each object.

 Measure each object using centimeters and meters.
Circle the unit you need fewer of to measure each object.

1.

about _____ centimeters   fewer centimeters

about _____ meters   fewer meters

2.

about _____ centimeters   fewer centimeters

about _____ meters   fewer meters

Topic 12 | Lesson 7   Digital Resources at SavvasRealize.com   seven hundred thirty-three **733**

3. Make Sense Circle the objects that are easier to measure using centimeters. Cross out the objects that are easier to measure using meters.

4. Higher Order Thinking Shane and Karen want to measure the length of a soccer field.
Should they use centimeters or meters to measure it? Explain.

_____

_____

_____

Think about the size of one unit.

5. ✓Assessment Carlos measures the length of a couch in centimeters and meters. How will his measurements compare?

Choose Yes or No.

more centimeters than meters ○ Yes ○ No

fewer centimeters than meters ○ Yes ○ No

fewer meters than centimeters ○ Yes ○ No

the same number of centimeters and meters ○ Yes ○ No

Independent Practice

Estimate the length of each path.
Then use a centimeter ruler to measure each path.

5.

Path C

Estimate: about _____ centimeters

Measure: about _____ centimeters

6.

Path D

Estimate: about _____ centimeters

Measure: about _____ centimeters

---

7. Which path is longer?

_____

8. How much longer?

about _____ centimeters longer

Higher Order Thinking Think about the length of each object.
Circle the best estimate of its length.

9. a key

about 1 cm   about 6 cm   about 20 cm

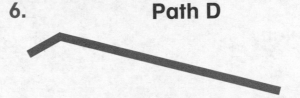

Think about objects that are about 1 cm long to help.

10. a pen

about 2 cm   about 4 cm   about 15 cm

Use your estimates to complete:

A pen is about _____ cm longer

than a _____.

11. **Explain** A path has two parts. The total length of the path is 12 cm. If one part is 8 cm, how long is the other part? Explain.

_____ centimeters

12. **Higher Order Thinking** Draw a path with two parts. Measure the length to the nearest centimeter. Write an equation to show the length of your path.

13. **Higher Order Thinking** Beth drew a picture of a bike path. Use tools. Measure the length of the path below. Write the total length.

Beth's Path

about _____ centimeters

14. ✓**Assessment** Peter measures a path that has a total length of 12 cm. Janna measures a path that has two parts. Each part measures 7 cm.

How much longer is Janna's path than Peter's path? Show your work.

_____

_____

_____

Name _____

Another Look! You can write an equation
to help you find the total length of a path.
What is the total length of Path A?

Path A

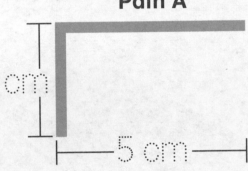

3 cm

5 cm

$3 + 5 = 8$

Measure each part of
a path to start.

HOME ACTIVITY Draw a
path that is made up of
two parts. Have your child
use a centimeter ruler to
measure each part and
then find the total length.

Path A is about ___8___ centimeters long.

Use a centimeter ruler to measure Path B. Answer each question.

I. **Path B**

____ + ____ = ____

about ____ centimeters long

2. Which path is longer,
Path A or Path B?

Path A

Path B

3. How much longer is the
longer path than the
shorter path?

about ____ centimeter
longer

4. Model Joanna drew a path that is 8 cm shorter than Liam's path. Joanna's path is 19 cm long. How long is Liam's path? Write an equation.

_____ + _____ = _____ centimeters

5. Model Nadine drew a path that is 7 cm longer than Nancy's path. Nadine's path is 15 cm long. How long is Nancy's path? Write an equation.

_____ – _____ = _____ centimeters

Use the pictures on the right to solve each problem.

6. Kristin cleans out her desk. Write the items she finds in order from longest to shortest. Then fill in the blanks for each sentence below.

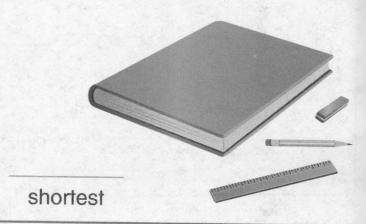

_____   _____   _____   _____

longest   shortest

7. Higher Order Thinking Fill in the missing words.

The pencil is _____ than the ruler,

and the ruler is shorter than the

_____ . So, the pencil is

_____ than the _____ .

8. ✅**Assessment** Use a ruler. What is the total length of the purple path?

Ⓐ about 2 centimeters

Ⓑ about 4 centimeters

Ⓒ about 6 centimeters

Ⓓ about 8 centimeters

Independent Practice ✫ Solve each problem.

2. Traci measures the length of her pencil.
   She uses a centimeter ruler.
   Traci writes 17 for the length.
   Is her answer precise? Explain.

   _____
   _____
   _____
   _____

3. Steve uses centimeter cubes. He says
   the pencil is 9 centimeters long. Is his
   work precise? Explain.

   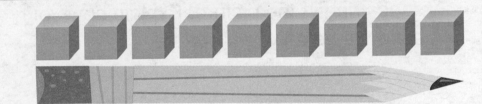

   _____
   _____

4. Use a centimeter ruler to measure the pencil yourself.
   How long is the pencil? Explain what you did to make sure
   your work is precise.

   _____
   _____
   _____

Shoestring

Katie lost a shoestring.
The shoestring has the same length as the shoestring at the right.
What is the length of the shoestring Katie lost?

5. **Make Sense** Estimate the length of the shoestring in the picture. Explain how your estimate helps you measure.

_____

_____

_____

_____

6. **Use Tools** What tools can you use to measure the shoestring? Explain.

_____

_____

_____

_____

7. **Be Precise** Measure the shoestring.
Tell why your work is precise.

_____

_____

_____

Name _____

Another Look! Amy uses a button to measure the length of a glue stick.

She knows one button is 1 centimeter. She finds that the glue stick is 5 cm.

Amy used a ruler to check her work. She started at the 0 mark.

HOME ACTIVITY Have your child measure the length of a household item. Have your child choose the unit to use. Ask your child to explain how he or she knows the measurement is precise.

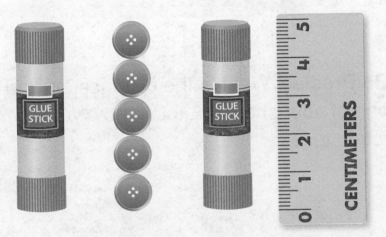

Amy got the same answer both times. So, she knows her work is precise! It helps to measure twice!

First time: 5 cm   **Second time: 5 cm**

Solve the problem. You can use string or buttons to help.

1. Find the length of the chain at the right.
   Estimate and use tools to measure.

   Estimate: _____

   Actual measurement: _____

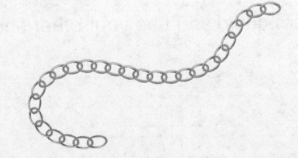

Distance Around Your Shoe

Shoes have different sizes and shapes.
The picture shows the bottom of a shoe.
What is the total distance around the bottom
of one of your shoes?

2. **Reasoning** What units of measure will
you use? Explain.

_____

_____

_____

_____

3. **Be Precise** What is the distance around
one of your shoes? Explain how you
found it.

_____

_____

_____

_____

_____

4. **Explain** How could you use your other shoe to check your work?

_____

_____

_____

Find a partner. Point to a clue. Read the clue.

Look below the clues to find a match. Write the clue letter in the box next to the match.

Find a match for every clue.

Find a Match

I can ...
add and subtract within 100.

Clues

A The sum is between 47 and 53.

B The difference equals 56 − 20.

C The sum equals 100.

D The difference equals 79 − 27.

E The difference is between 25 and 35.

F The sum equals 41 + 56.

G The difference is less than 20.

H The sum equals 26 + 19.

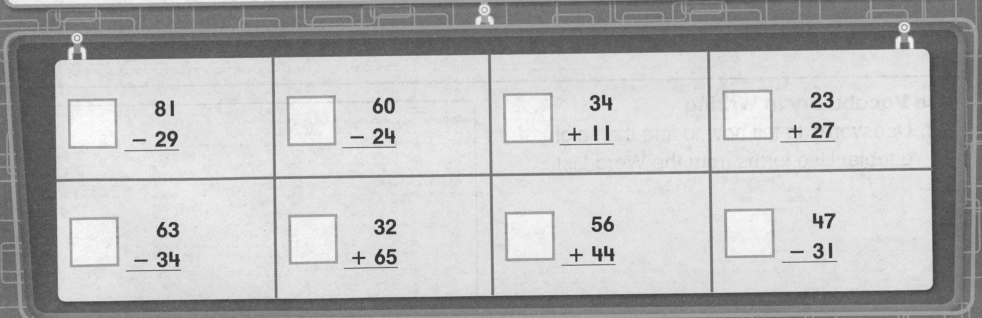

	81 − 29		60 − 24		34 + 11		23 + 27
	63 − 34		32 + 65		56 + 44		47 − 31

A-Z Glossary

Word List
- centimeter (cm)
- estimate
- foot (ft)
- height
- inch (in.)
- length
- meter (m)
- nearest centimeter
- nearest inch
- yard (yd)

Understand Vocabulary

I. Circle the unit that has the *greatest* length.

foot   meter   inch

2. Circle the unit that has the *shortest* length.

yard   inch   centimeter

3. Cross out the unit you would **NOT** use to measure the length of a book.

inch   centimeter   yard

4. Cross out the unit you would **NOT** use to measure the height of a house.

inch   foot   meter

Estimate the length of each item.

5. pencil

_____

6. paper clip

_____

7. school desk

_____

Use Vocabulary in Writing

8. Use words to tell how to find the height of a table. Use terms from the Word List.

_____

_____

_____

_____

Set A

There are 12 inches in 1 foot.
There are 3 feet in 1 yard.
You can use lengths of objects you know to estimate lengths of other objects.

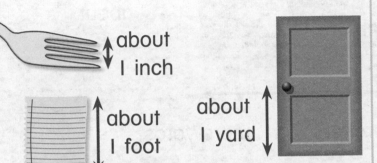

about 1 inch

about 1 foot

about 1 yard

Estimate the lengths of two classroom objects in feet. Name each object and write your estimate.

1. Object: _____

about _____ feet

2. Object: _____

about _____ feet

Set B

You can measure the length of an object to the nearest inch.

INCHES

halfway mark

The string is longer than halfway between 1 and 2.
So, use the greater number.
The string is about __2__ inches.

Find objects like the ones shown. Use a ruler to measure their lengths.

3.

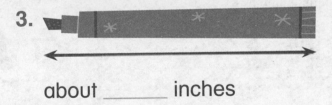

about _____ inches

4.

about _____ inches

The measure of the height of a window takes *more* feet than yards.

about __3__ feet

about __1__ yard

Measure the object in inches and feet. Circle the unit you needed *more* of.

5.

about _____ feet

about _____ yards

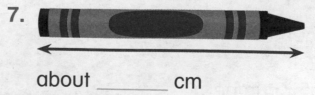

more feet   more yards

You can measure the length of an object to the nearest centimeter.

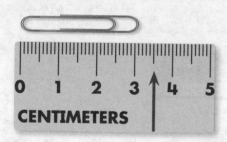

The paper clip is less than halfway between 3 and 4.
So, use the lesser number.
The paper clip is about __3__ cm.

Find objects like the ones shown. Use a ruler to measure their lengths.

6.

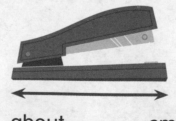

about _____ cm

7.

about _____ cm

Name _____

Set E

There are 100 centimeters in
1 meter.

about 1 centimeter

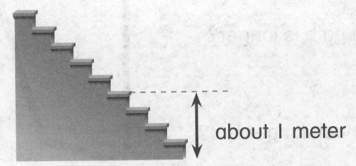

about 1 meter

Circle the picture of the object that
is about each length or height.

Reteaching
Continued

8. about 1 centimeter

9. about 1 meter

Set F

The measure of the height of this cart
takes *fewer* meters than centimeters.

about __93__ centimeters

about __1__ meter

Measure the object in centimeters and meters.
Circle the unit you needed *fewer* of.

10.

about _____ centimeters

about _____ meters

fewer centimeters

fewer meters

Which path is longer? How much longer?
Measure each part. Then add the lengths.

$4 + 2 = 6$

The purple path
is 6 cm.

$2 + 3 = 5$

The green path
is 5 cm.

Subtract the lengths to compare.

$6 - 5 = 1$

The purple path is

about 1 centimeter longer.

Thinking Habits

Attend to Precision

Which unit of measure will I use?

Is my work precise?

Use a centimeter ruler. Measure each path.

11. Red path: _____ centimeters

12. Blue path: _____ centimeters

13. Which path is longer?

_____

How much longer is it?

about _____ centimeters longer

14. Measure the length of the bottom of this page in feet and in inches.

about _____ ft   about _____ in.

15. Which measure in Item 14 is more precise? Explain.

_____

_____

_____

Name _____

1. Estimate. About how tall is the flower?

Ⓐ about 5 cm

Ⓑ about 10 cm

Ⓒ about 15 cm

Ⓓ about 1 meter

I cm

2. Draw a line from each estimate to a matching object.

about
1 inch

about
1 foot

about
1 yard

3. Which units would you need the fewest of to measure the height of a fence?

Ⓐ inches

Ⓑ feet

Ⓒ yards

Ⓓ all the same

4. Dan measures the width of the window with a yardstick. He says it measures 3. Is his answer precise? Explain.

_____

_____

_____

_____

5. Use a ruler to measure each line to the nearest centimeter.
Which are about 3 centimeters long? Choose all that apply.

☐ ─────────

☐ ────────

☐ ──────

☐ ───────

6. Use a ruler to measure the length of the pencil in inches.
Which is the correct measurement?

Ⓐ 2 inches

Ⓑ 3 inches

Ⓒ 4 inches

Ⓓ 5 inches

7. Circle the unit you need fewer of to measure the length of a kitchen.

fewer centimeters   fewer meters

Circle the unit you need fewer of to measure the length of a table.

fewer feet   fewer yards

8. Use a ruler. Measure each path to the nearest inch.

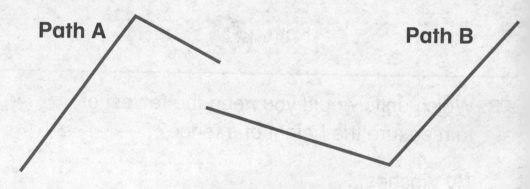

Path A

Path B

Which path is longer? _____

How much longer? about _____ longer

9. Use a ruler. Measure the length of the marker to the nearest centimeter.
How long is the marker?

Ⓐ 6 centimeters

Ⓑ 9 centimeters

Ⓒ 12 centimeters

Ⓓ 15 centimeters

10. A path has two parts.
The total length of the path is 15 cm.
One part of the path is 9 cm long.
How long is the other part?

Ⓐ 24 cm

Ⓑ 15 cm

Ⓒ 9 cm

Ⓓ 6 cm

11. Use a ruler. Measure each path to the nearest centimeter.

Path A

Path B

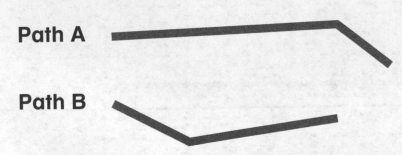

Which path is longer? _____

How much longer?

about _____ longer

12. Measure the gray line with tools you need to be precise. Choose all the measurements that are precise.

☐ 4 centimeters

☐ 4 inches

☐ 10

☐ 10 centimeters

13. Juan uses different units to measure a jump rope. Compare the measurements.

Choose Yes or No.

more inches than feet ○ Yes ○ No

fewer inches than feet ○ Yes ○ No

more centimeters than meters ○ Yes ○ No

fewer centimeters than meters ○ Yes ○ No

14. Kendra measures her crayon to the nearest centimeter.
What is the length of her crayon to the nearest centimeter?

CENTIMETERS

_____ centimeters

15. Kim's softball bat is 1 yard long.
She uses 3 bats to measure the length of the classroom whiteboard.
About how long is the whiteboard?

3 inches   3 feet   1 yard   3 yards
Ⓐ   Ⓑ   Ⓒ   Ⓓ

16. Kevin measured the length of a car in inches and in feet. Why is the number of feet less than the number of inches?

96 inches or 8 feet

Name _____

Happy Hiking!
The Torres family loves to hike.
They use this map to plan their hiking trip.

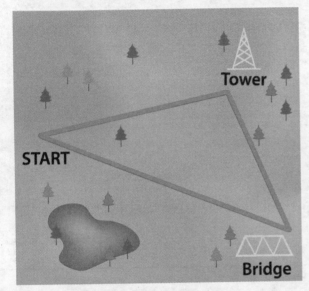

1. Use a centimeter ruler.
Find the total length of the triangle
hiking path shown on the map.

about _____ centimeters

Explain how you found the length.

_____

_____

_____

2. Debbie Torres uses a backpack
for hiking.
She wants to measure its length.
She wants to be precise. Should she
use inches, feet, or yards?
Explain your answer.

Length of a backpack

_____

_____

_____

_____

3. Daniel Torres estimates the height of his water bottle. Is his estimate reasonable? Explain.

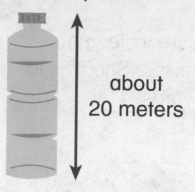

about 20 meters

_____

_____

_____

_____

4. Maria Torres says that it would take more yards than feet to measure the height of the tower. Do you agree? Circle Yes or No. Then explain why.

Yes   No

_____

_____

_____

5. On the hike, the Torres family sees a caterpillar. Use the picture below to answer the questions.

Part A

To be precise, which unit would you choose to measure the length of the caterpillar?

_____

_____

Part B

Estimate and then measure the length of the caterpillar. Then explain how you measured.

Estimate: _____

Measurement: _____

_____

_____

_____

_____

Topic 12 | Performance Assessment

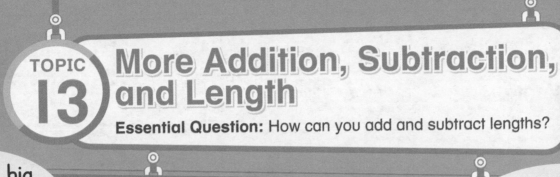

Digital Resources

Solve Learn Glossary

Tools Assessment Help Games

Look at the big waves! Look at the big rock!

Water and land in an area can have different sizes and shapes.

Wow! Let's do this project and learn more.

Math and Science Project: Modeling Land, Water, and Length

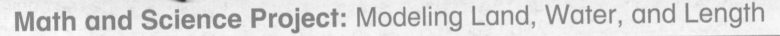

Find Out Find and share books and other sources that show the shapes and kinds of land and water in an area. Draw a picture or make a model to show the land or water in an area.

Journal: Make a Book Show what you learn in a book. In your book, also:

• Draw a picture to show the shape of some land or water in your area.

• Make up a math story about lengths. Draw a picture to show how to solve the problem in your story.

Name _____

Review What You Know

A-Z Vocabulary

1. Circle the measuring unit that is better to **estimate** the **length** of a room.

   meter

   centimeter

2. Circle the number of feet in 1 **yard**.

   2 feet

   3 feet

   4 feet

   12 feet

3. The clock shows the time a math class begins. Circle **a.m.** or **p.m.**

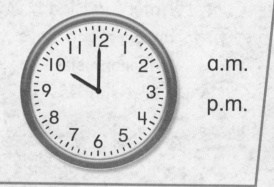

   a.m.

   p.m.

Estimate

4. **Estimate** the length of the eraser in centimeters.

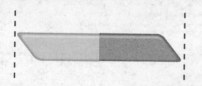

   About _____ centimeters

Compare

5. A sidewalk is 632 yards long. A jogging trail is 640 yards long.

   Use <, >, or = to compare the lengths.

   632 ◯ 640

Rectangles

6. Label the 2 missing lengths of the sides of the rectangle.

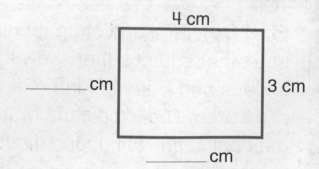

   4 cm

   _____ cm

   3 cm

   _____ cm

Name _____

Solve & Share

What is the total distance around the blue rectangle in centimeters? Show your work. Did you add or subtract?

I can ...
solve problems by adding or subtracting length measurements.

I can also be precise in my work.

_____ ◯ _____ ◯ _____ ◯ _____ = _____

The distance around the blue rectangle is _____ centimeters.

The book is 9 inches long and 6 inches wide.

What is the distance around the front cover of the book?

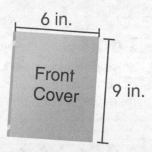

6 in.

Front Cover

9 in.

Add the lengths of all four sides to find the distance around the cover.

$9 + 6 + 9 + 6 = ?$

$18 + 12 =$

$10 + 10 + 8 + 2 =$

$20 + 10 = 30$

The distance around the cover is 30 inches.

Think: Will I add or subtract?

How much longer is the teacher's arm than the child's arm?

Arm Length in Centimeters	
Teacher	66
Child	47

Subtract to compare measurements.

$66 - 47 = ?$

$$\begin{array}{r} 5\,16 \\ \cancel{6}\,\cancel{6} \\ -\;4\,7 \\ \hline 19 \end{array}$$

The teacher's arm is 19 centimeters longer than the child's arm.

Do You Understand?

Show Me! Explain how to find the distance around a square park that is 2 miles long on each side.

☆ Guided Practice ☆

Decide if you need to add or subtract. Then write an equation to help solve each problem.

1. What is the distance around the baseball card?

$10 + 7 + 10 + 7 = 34$

Distance around: __34__ cm

10 cm

7 cm

2. What is the distance around the puzzle?

_____

Distance around: _____ in.

15 in.

12 in.

Topic 13 | Lesson 1

★ Independent ★ Practice

Decide if you need to add or subtract.
Then write an equation to help solve each problem.

3. What is the distance around the door?

_____

Distance around: _____ ft

3 ft

7 ft

4. What is the distance around the cell phone?

_____

Distance around: _____ in.

2 in.

4 in.

5. How much longer is the red scarf than the blue scarf?

_____

_____ in. longer

60 in.

45 in.

6. Algebra What is the length of the shorter side of the rectangle? Complete the equation to solve.

20 + _____ + 20 + _____ = 60

The shorter side is _____ centimeters.

20 cm

?

Decide if you need to add or subtract.
Then write an equation to help solve each problem.

An equation is a model.

7. **Model** Ashley's sunflower is 70 inches tall. Kwame's sunflower is 60 inches tall. How much taller is Ashley's sunflower than Kwame's sunflower?

70 in.   60 in.

_____ _____ inches taller

8. **Model** Ben measures the length of a leaf and a plant. The leaf is 15 centimeters. The plant is 37 centimeters. How much shorter is the leaf than the plant?

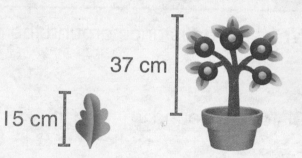

37 cm

15 cm

_____ _____ centimeters shorter

9. **Higher Order Thinking** Tyler threw a ball 42 feet and then 44 feet. Sanjay threw a ball 38 feet and then 49 feet. Who threw the longer distance in all? Show your work.

10. ✓**Assessment** What is the distance around the placemat?

Ⓐ 28 in.

Ⓑ 39 in.

Ⓒ 56 in.

Ⓓ 66 in.

11 in.

17 in.

Topic 13 | Lesson

Name _____

Another Look!

You can use addition or subtraction to solve problems with measurements. How much longer is the snake than the worm?

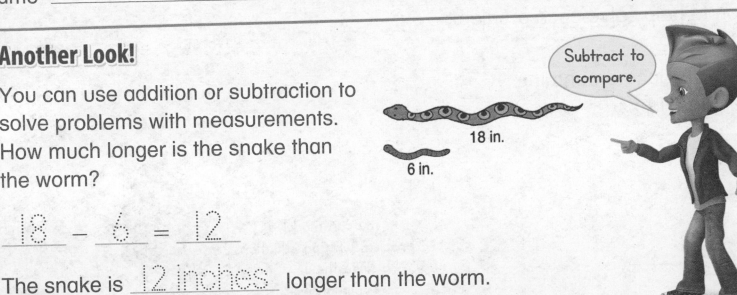

Subtract to compare.

18 in.

6 in.

$\underline{18} - \underline{6} = \underline{12}$

The snake is ___12 inches___ longer than the worm.

HOME ACTIVITY Ask your child to find a rectangular object (*a book, piece of paper, tile, etc.*). Have your child measure each side in inches and write an equation to find the distance around the object.

Decide if you need to add or subtract.
Then write an equation to help solve each problem.

1. How much shorter is the feather than the ribbon?

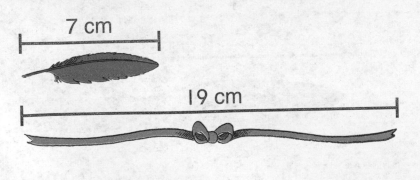

7 cm

19 cm

_____ centimeters shorter

2. What is the distance around the rug?

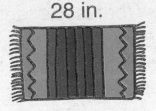

28 in.

15 in.

_____

_____ inches

Decide if you need to add or subtract.
Then write an equation to help solve each problem.

3. **Model** What is the distance around the front cover of the game box?

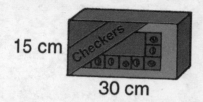

15 cm

30 cm

_____

The distance around the game

box is _____ .

You can model a problem with an equation. Include the units in your answer.

4. **Higher Order Thinking** The distance around Tim's rectangular book is 48 centimeters. The length of each longer side is 14 cm. What is the length of each shorter side? Show your work.

_____

_____

Each shorter side of the book is

_____ long.

5. ✓**Assessment** How much longer is the green fish than the blue fish?

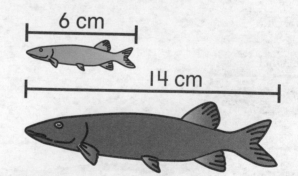

6 cm

14 cm

Ⓐ 7 cm

Ⓑ 8 cm

Ⓒ 20 cm

Ⓓ 40 cm

Name _____

Solve & Share

Julie and Steve each cut a piece of yarn.
The total length of both pieces is 12 cm.

Use centimeter cubes to measure each piece of yarn.
Circle Julie and Steve's pieces. Then explain your thinking.

I can ...
add or subtract to solve
problems about measurements.

I can also make math
arguments.

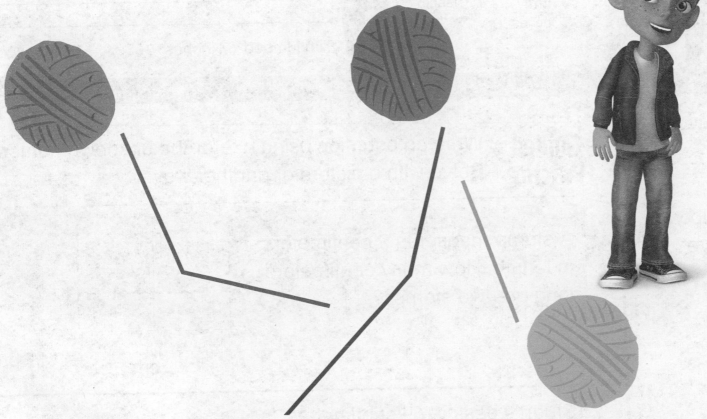

_____

_____

_____

Michelle jumped 24 inches. Tim jumped 7 fewer inches than Michelle. How far did Tim jump?

What operation should I use?

You can write a subtraction equation to show the problem.

The length of Tim's jump is unknown.

$$24 - 7 = ?$$

length of Michelle's jump | fewer inches | length of Tim's jump

You can draw a picture, such as a yardstick. Then count back to solve the problem.

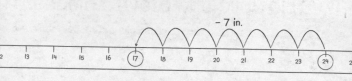

Tim jumped 17 inches.

Do You Understand?

Show Me! How does drawing a yardstick help you solve the problem above?

Guided Practice

Write an equation using a ? for the unknown number. Solve with a picture or another way.

1. A stamp measures 2 centimeters in length. How many centimeters long are two stamps?

$$2 + 2 = ?$$

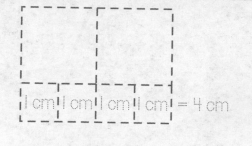

_____ cm

2. Stuart's desk is 64 centimeters long. His dresser is 7 centimeters longer than his desk. How long is Stuart's dresser?

_____ cm

Topic 13 | Lesson 2

Name _____

☆ **Independent Practice** — Write an equation using a ? for the unknown number. Solve with a picture or another way.

3. Filipe's pencil box is 24 centimeters long. Joe's pencil box is 3 centimeters shorter than Filipe's. How long is Joe's pencil box?

_____   _____ cm

4. Clark threw a red ball and a blue ball. He threw the red ball 17 feet. He threw the blue ball 7 feet farther. How far did Clark throw the blue ball?

_____   _____ ft

5. **Math and Science** Ashlie's map shows where animals, land, and water are at a zoo.

The distance around her map is 38 inches. What is the length of the missing side?

_____

_____ inches

8 in.

11 in.   ? in.

8 in.

6. Make Sense A brown puppy is 43 centimeters tall. A spotted puppy is 7 centimeters shorter than the brown puppy. A white puppy is 14 centimeters taller than the brown puppy. How tall is the spotted puppy? Think about what you need to find.

_____ cm

7. A-Z Vocabulary Complete the sentences using the terms below.

foot	**yard**	**inch**

A paper clip is about 1 _____ long.

My math book is about 1 _____ long.

A baseball bat is about 1 _____ long.

8. Higher Order Thinking Jack jumped 15 inches. Tyler jumped 1 inch less than Jack and 2 inches more than Randy. Who jumped the farthest? How far did each person jump?

9. Assessment Kim was 48 inches tall in January. She grew 9 inches during the year. How tall is Kim at the end of the year? Write an equation with an unknown and then draw a picture to solve.

_____ in.

Another Look!

Lance's boat is 13 meters long.
Cory's boat is 7 meters longer.
How long is Cory's boat?

You can follow these steps to solve word problems.

You can draw a picture to help.

Step 1 Write an equation to show the problem. $13 + 7 = ?$

Step 2 Draw a picture to help solve.

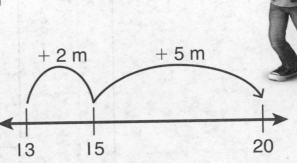

+ 2 m   + 5 m

13   15   20

Step 3 Solve the problem. Cory's boat is 20 meters long.

HOME ACTIVITY Have your child draw a picture to solve this problem. *A building is 24 meters tall. The tree next to the building is 5 meters tall. How much shorter is the tree than the building?*

Write an equation using a ? for the unknown number. Solve with a picture or another way.

1. Suzy's ribbon is 83 centimeters long.
   She cuts off 15 centimeters. How long is
   Suzy's ribbon now?

   _____   _____ cm

Solve each problem.

2. Jackie's shoelaces are 13 inches, 29 inches, and 58 inches long. What is the total length of all of Jackie's shoelaces? Draw a picture and write an equation to solve.

_____ in.

3. **Reasoning** Mary is 2 inches taller than Bill. Bill is 48 inches tall. How tall is Mary?

4. **Higher Order Thinking** Kyle's bedroom is 11 feet long. Garrett's bedroom is 2 feet longer than Kyle's room. Priya's bedroom is 3 feet shorter than Garrett's room. What is the sum of the lengths of Garrett and Priya's bedrooms?

_____ ft

5. **Assessment** Ryan's desk is 25 inches tall. His floor lamp is 54 inches tall. How many inches taller is Ryan's floor lamp? Write an equation and draw a picture to solve.

_____ inches taller

Name _____

Solve & Share

Alex has a piece of ribbon that is 45 feet long. He cuts the ribbon. Now he has 39 feet of ribbon. How many feet of ribbon did Alex cut off?

Draw a picture and write an equation to solve. Show your work.

I can ...
add and subtract to solve measurement problems by using drawings and equations.

I can also model with math.

_____ ◯ _____ = _____

A string is 28 cm.
Alex cuts off a piece.
Now the string is 16 cm.
How long is the piece of
string Alex cut off?

You can write an addition
or subtraction equation.

$$28 \quad - \quad ? \quad = \quad 16$$

↑   ↑   ↑
length   length   length
at first   cut   now

$$16 \quad + \quad ? \quad = \quad 28$$

↓   ↓   ↓
length   length   length
now   cut   at first

You can draw a picture for 28 − ? = 16 or 16 + ? = 28.

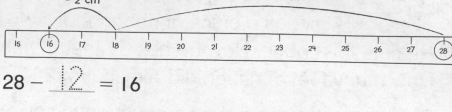

$$28 - \underline{12} = 16$$

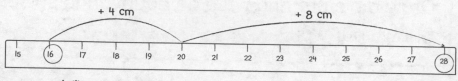

$$16 + \underline{12} = 28$$

Alex cut off 12 cm of string.

Do You Understand?

Show Me! How does writing
an equation help you solve
the problem above?

☆ Guided Practice ☆

Write an equation using a ? for the unknown
number. Solve with a picture or another way.

1. A plant was 15 inches tall.
   It grew and is now 22 inches
   tall. How many inches did the
   plant grow?

   $$15 + ? = 22$$

   + 5 in.   + 2 in.

   14 15 16 17 18 19 20 21 22 23

2. Each bus is 10 meters long.
   Each boat is 7 meters long.
   What is the total length of two
   buses and two boats?

Topic 13 | Lesson 3

Independent Practice

Write an equation using a ? for the unknown number.
Solve with a picture or another way.

3. Brent's rope is 49 inches long. He cuts off
some of the rope and now it is 37 inches long.
How much rope did Brent cut off?

_____   _____

4. Sue ran for some meters and stopped. Then
she ran another 22 meters for a total of
61 meters in all. How many meters did she run
at first?

_____   _____

5. **Algebra** Solve each equation. Use the chart.

◯	=	12
☆	=	39
△	=	42
☐	=	57

◯ + ☆ = _____

☐ − ☆ = _____

☆ + △ + ◯ = _____

6. Make Sense The yellow boat is 15 feet shorter than the green boat. The green boat is 53 feet long. How long is the yellow boat? Think about what you are trying to find.

Write an equation to solve. Show your work.

_____ ft

7. 🅐🅩 **Vocabulary** Steve measured the length of his desk. It measured 2 units.

Circle the unit Steve used.

meter   foot   centimeter   inch

Lori measured the length of her cat. It measured 45 units.

Circle the unit Lori used.

centimeter   yard   inch   foot

8. Higher Order Thinking Lucy's ribbon is 1 foot long. Kathleen's ribbon is 15 inches long. Whose ribbon is longer and by how many inches? Explain your thinking.

_____

_____

_____

9. ✅ **Assessment** Mary's water bottle is 25 cm long. Joey's water bottle is 22 cm long. Ella's water bottle is 17 cm long.

Which statements are correct? Choose all that apply.

☐ Mary's bottle is 8 cm longer than Ella's.

☐ Joey's bottle is 6 cm longer than Ella's.

☐ Joey's bottle is 3 cm shorter than Mary's.

☐ Ella's bottle is 8 cm longer than Mary's.

Name _____

Another Look!

Kelsey is 59 inches tall.

She grows and is now 73 inches tall.

How many inches did Kelsey grow?

Show the problem with an equation: $59 + ? = 73$.

You can draw a picture of a tape measure to solve the problem.

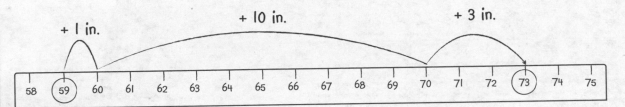

+ 1 in.   + 10 in.   + 3 in.

58 59 60 61 62 63 64 65 66 67 68 69 70 71 72 73 74 75

Kelsey grew 14 inches.

HOME ACTIVITY Have your child draw a picture and write an equation to solve this problem. *Paul has 45 feet of string. Sal cuts some string off. Now Paul has 38 feet of string. How many feet of string did Sal cut off?*

Write an equation using a ? for the unknown number. Solve with a picture or another way.

1. Brigit has a piece of rope. She ties 18 more meters of rope to her rope. Now the rope is 27 meters long. How long was the rope to begin with?

_____   _____

Topic 13 | Lesson 3   Digital Resources at SavvasRealize.com   seven hundred seventy-seven **777**

Solve each problem.

Remember to use the correct words and symbols to explain your thinking.

2. **Explain** Elizabeth ran 36 meters.
Haruki ran 8 fewer meters than Elizabeth.
Delilah ran 3 fewer meters than Haruki.
How many meters did Delilah run?
Explain your thinking.

_____

_____

_____

3. **Higher Order Thinking** The lengths of the pencils are given at the right.

Write and solve a two-step problem about the pencils.

_____

_____

_____

_____

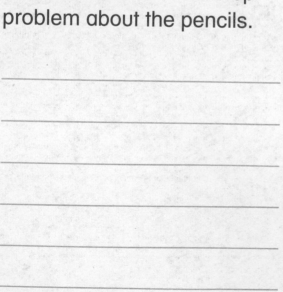

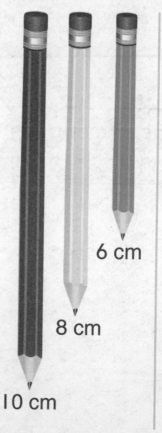

6 cm

8 cm

10 cm

4. ✓**Assessment** A hammer is 1 foot long. A car is 15 feet long. A shovel is 4 feet long.

Which statements are correct? Choose all that apply.

☐ The car is 9 ft longer than the hammer.

☐ The hammer is 14 ft shorter than the car.

☐ The shovel is 3 ft longer than the hammer.

☐ The car is 11 feet longer than the shovel.

778 seven hundred seventy-eight

Independent Practice ✩ Use the number lines to add or subtract.

3. $80 - 35 =$ _____

4. $19 + 63 =$ _____

5. Higher Order Thinking Use the number line to show 15 inches plus 0 inches. Explain your thinking.

_____

_____

6. Number Sense Show each number below as a length from 0 on the number line. Draw four separate arrows.

 9   14   24   28

7. Use Tools A football team gains 15 yards on its first play. The team gains 12 yards on its second play. How many yards does the team gain in two plays?

_____ yards

8. Use Tools Mia buys 25 feet of board. She uses 16 feet of board for a sandbox. How many feet of board does she have left?

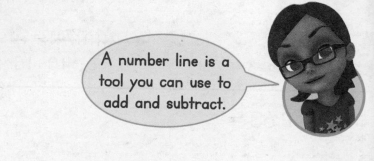

A number line is a tool you can use to add and subtract.

_____ feet

9. Higher Order Thinking The runners on the track team ran 12 miles on Monday. On Tuesday, they ran 6 more miles than they ran on Monday. How many miles did they run in all on both days?

_____ miles

10. ✅Assessment Deb has two pencils. One pencil is 9 cm long and the other pencil is 13 cm long. What is the total length of both pencils?

Use the number line to show your work.

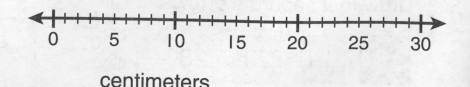

_____ centimeters

Help Tools Games

Another Look! What tool would you use to solve this problem?

Valerie drives 21 miles on Monday and 49 miles on Tuesday. How many miles does she drive in all?

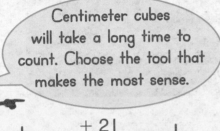

Centimeter cubes will take a long time to count. Choose the tool that makes the most sense.

You can draw a number line to solve this problem.

HOME ACTIVITY Ask your child to explain what tool he or she would use to solve this problem: *Measure the length of a door and a window to the nearest foot. How much longer is the door than the window?*

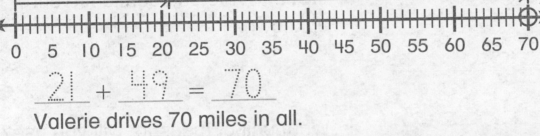

+ 21   + 49

0   5   10 15 20 25 30 35 40 45 50 55 60 65 70

21 + 49 = 70

Valerie drives 70 miles in all.

Choose a tool to help you solve the problem. Show your work. Explain why you chose that tool and how you got your answer.

1. Aaron was 38 inches tall when he was 4 years old. Aaron is 8 years old and 47 inches tall. How many inches did Aaron grow?

Trains

Mr. Bolt needs to measure the length of a train.
The first car is the engine car. It is 8 meters long.
There are also four boxcars. Each boxcar is
12 meters long.

Help Mr. Bolt find the total length of the train.

2. **Make Sense** What information is given?
What do you need to find?

_____

_____

_____

_____

3. **Model** Write an equation to show the unknown.

_____

What unit of measure will you use?

_____

4. **Use Tools** What is the total length of the train?
Choose a tool to solve the problem. Show your work. _____

Name _____

Set A

What is the distance around the front of the bookcase?

4 ft

3 ft

Write an equation to help solve.

1. What is the distance around the front of the crayon box?

12 cm

9 cm

Opposite sides have equal measures.

Add the lengths. Write an equation.

$4 + 3 + 4 + 3 = \underline{14}$

Distance around: __14__ feet

Distance around: _____ cm

Set B

A kite string is 27 feet long.
Some of the string is cut off.
Now the kite string is 18 feet long.
How many feet of kite string were cut off?

Write an equation and draw a picture.

$27 - ? = 18$ or $18 + ? = 27$

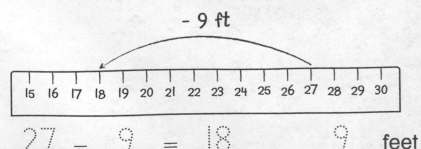

- 9 ft

| 15 | 16 | 17 | 18 | 19 | 20 | 21 | 22 | 23 | 24 | 25 | 26 | 27 | 28 | 29 | 30 |

__27__ − __9__ = __18__   __9__ feet

Write an equation using a symbol, ?, for the unknown number. Then draw a picture to solve.

2. A piece of yarn is 42 inches long. Mia cuts some of it off. It is now 26 inches long. How much yarn did Mia cut off?

_____

A book measures 10 inches long. Another book measures 13 inches long. What is the total length of both books?

You can show $10 + 13$ on a number line.

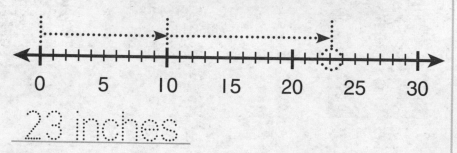

23 inches

Solve the problem using the number line.

3. One room in Jackie's house is 15 feet long. Another room is 9 feet long. What is the total length of both rooms?

_____

Thinking Habits

Use Tools

Which of these tools can I use?

counters   paper and pencil
cubes   place-value blocks
measuring tools   technology
number line

Am I using the tool correctly?

Choose a tool to solve the problem.

4. Damon's shoelace is 45 inches long. His shoelace breaks. One piece is 28 inches long. How long is the other piece?

Explain your solution and why you chose the tool you used.

_____ ◯ _____ = _____ _____

Name _____

1. What is the distance around the cover of the notepad?

7 in.

5 in.

Distance around: _____ in.

2. Kate is 48 inches tall. Tom is 2 inches taller than Kate. James is 3 inches shorter than Tom.

How tall is James?

Ⓐ   45 inches   Ⓒ   50 inches

Ⓑ   47 inches   Ⓓ   53 inches

3. Alexis has a rope that is 7 feet long. Mariah's rope is 9 feet long. Sam's rope is 3 feet longer than Mariah's rope.

Use the measurements on the cards to complete each sentence.

| 2 feet | 5 feet | 12 feet |

Sam's rope is _____ long.

Alexis's rope is _____ shorter than Mariah's rope.

Sam's rope is _____ longer than Alexis's rope.

4. Joe rides his bike 18 miles. Then he rides 7 more miles.

Use the number line to find how far Joe rides. Then explain your work.

0   5   10   15   20   25   30

5. Pat says that each unknown equals 25 cm. Do you agree? Choose Yes or No.

47 cm + ? = 72 cm   ○ Yes ○ No

? + 39 cm = 54 cm   ○ Yes ○ No

99 cm − 64 cm = ?   ○ Yes ○ No

93 cm − ? = 68 cm   ○ Yes ○ No

6. Grace got a plant that was 34 cm tall. The plant grew and now it is 42 cm tall. How many centimeters did the plant grow?

Ⓐ 8 cm

Ⓑ 12 cm

Ⓒ 42 cm

Ⓓ 76 cm

7. Claire rides her bike 26 miles on Saturday and Sunday. She rides 8 miles on Sunday. How many miles does she ride on Saturday?

Write an equation to show the unknown.
Then use the number line to solve the problem.

_____ miles

8. Chris had a string that is 18 cm long. He cut off 7 cm. How much string is left?

Part A Which of these tools could you use to solve the problem? Choose all that apply.

☐ centimeter ruler

☐ paper and pencil

☐ number line

☐ inch ruler

Part B Write an equation to show the unknown. Then draw a number line to solve.

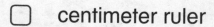

_____ cm

Topic 13 | Assessment

Name _____

Fishing Fun

Jim and his family go on a fishing trip.
They use a boat and fishing gear to help
them catch fish.

1. Jim takes this fishing box with him.
   What is the distance around the front
   of the fishing box? Write an equation
   to help solve the problem.

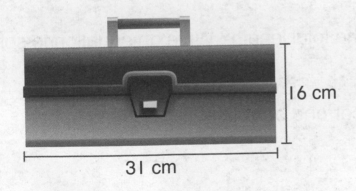

16 cm

31 cm

Distance around: _____ centimeters

2. Jim's fishing pole is 38 inches long.
   His dad's fishing pole is 96 inches
   long. How much shorter is Jim's
   pole than his dad's pole?

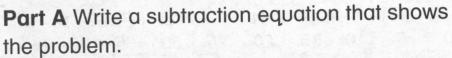

   Part A Write a subtraction equation that shows
   the problem.

   _____

   Part B Solve the problem.

   _____ inches shorter

3. Jim catches a fish 49 yards away from the shore.
   Later, he helps row the boat closer to the shore.
   Now he is 27 yards away from the shore.
   How many yards closer to shore is Jim now than
   when he caught the fish?

   Part A Write an addition equation that shows the
   problem.

   _____

   Part B Solve the problem.

   _____ yards

4. Jim catches a silver fish that is 12 inches long. His sister catches a green fish that is 27 inches long.

What is the total length of both fish? Use the number line to solve.

_____ inches

5. Jim has 27 yards of fishing line. He gives 12 yards of line to a friend. How many yards of line does Jim have left?

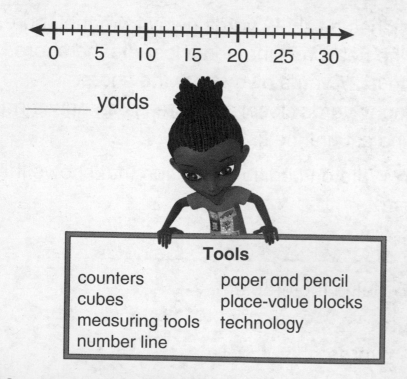

_____ yards

Tools

counters   paper and pencil
cubes   place-value blocks
measuring tools   technology
number line

6. Jim's family meets a man with a big boat. A parking spot at the dock is 32 feet long. Will the man's car and boat fit in the parking spot?

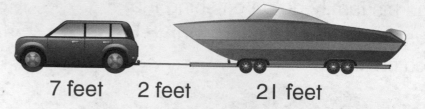

7 feet   2 feet   21 feet

Part A
What do you need to find? _____

_____

_____

Part B
What is the total length? Write an equation to solve.

_____   _____

Will the car and boat fit in the parking spot? Explain.

_____

_____

What tool did you use? _____

Topic 13 | Performance Assessment

Graphs and Data

Essential Question: How can line plots, bar graphs, and picture graphs be used to show data and answer questions?

These backpacks look cool!

But which one would work better for you?

Wow! Let's do this project and learn more.

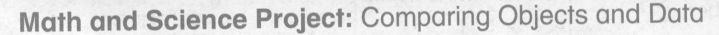

Math and Science Project: Comparing Objects and Data

Find Out Work with a partner. Compare two backpacks. Which one holds more? Which one has more parts? Which one is easier to put on? Think of other ways to compare.

Journal: Make a Book Show what you learn in a book. In your book, also:

- Tell one good thing and one bad thing about each backpack.

- Draw line plots, picture graphs, and bar graphs to show and compare data.

Name _____

Review What You Know

Vocabulary

1. Circle the number that has a 6 in the **tens** place.

406

651

160

2. Circle the **tally marks** that show 6.

Favorite Toy	
Car	卌 ll
Blocks	llll
Doll	卌 l

3. Circle the **difference**.

$$22 - 9 = 13$$

$$34 + 61 = 95$$

Comparing Numbers

4. A zoo has 405 snakes. It has 375 monkeys. Compare the number of snakes to the number of monkeys.

Write > or <.

405 ◯ 375

Interpret Data

5.

Picnic Tickets Sold	
Jean	16
Paulo	18
Fatima	12

Who sold the most picnic tickets?

_____

Addition and Subtraction

6. Byron scores 24 points in a game.
Ava scores 16 points in the same game.
How many more points does Byron score than Ava?

_____ more points

My Word Cards

Study the words on the front of the card.
Complete the activity on the back.

A-Z Glossary

data

Favorite Fruit	
Apple	7
Peach	4
Orange	5

line plot

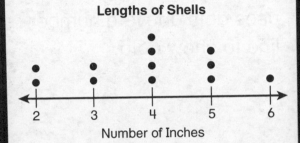

Lengths of Shells

Number of Inches

bar graph

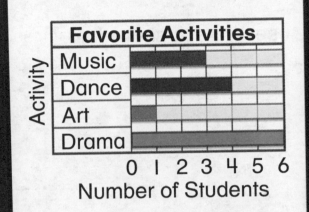

symbol

A 🤸 stands for 1 student.

Some math symbols: = + −

picture graph

Favorite Ball Games	
Baseball	🤸 🤸
Soccer	🤸 🤸 🤸 🤸 🤸 🤸 🤸
Tennis	🤸 🤸 🤸 🤸

Each 🤸 = 1 student

My Word Cards

Use what you know to complete the sentences.
Extend learning by writing your own sentence using each word.

A ____________________

uses bars to show data.

A ____________________

uses dots above a number line to show data.

____

are information you collect.

A ____________________

____

uses pictures to show data.

A ____________________

is a picture or character that stands for something.

Name _____

Another Look! You can make a line plot to show data.

The table shows the lengths of objects in inches.
Use the data from the table to make a line plot.

HOME ACTIVITY Use the line plot to ask your child questions about the data. Encourage your child to explain each answer.

Object	Length in Inches
Pencil	5
Scissors	8
Stapler	6

Lengths of Objects

The line plot helps you see which object is shortest and which one is longest.

Number of Inches

 Use the line plot above to answer the questions.

1. Which object is longest? _____

2. Which object is shortest? _____

3. How much shorter is the stapler than the scissors? _____

4. How much longer is the scissors than the pencil? _____

Be Precise Measure each shoe in inches. Then record each length in the table. Show each length on the line plot.

5. The green shoe is _____ long.

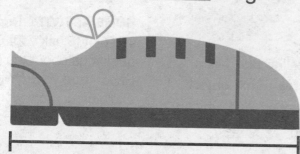

6. The purple shoe is _____ long.

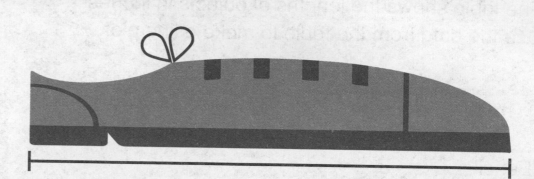

7.

Shoe Color	Length in Inches
Blue	4
Red	5
Green	
Purple	

Lengths of Shoes

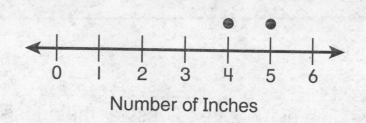

Number of Inches

8. Higher Order Thinking Which three shoes have a total length of 13 inches? Explain.

_____

_____

_____

9. ✓**Assessment** Measure the length of the yellow shoe in inches. Write the length below. Record your measurement on the line plot above.

_____

Independent Practice

Collect data and use the data to complete the line plot. Then use the line plot to solve the problems.

4. Measure the length of your pencil in centimeters. Collect pencil-length data from your classmates. Make a line plot with the data.

Title: _____

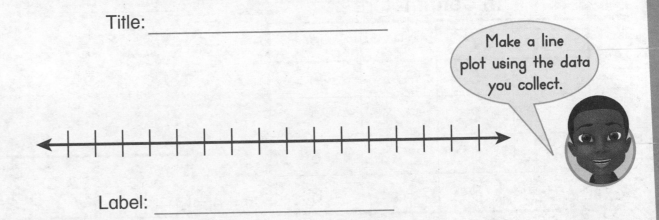

Label: _____

Make a line plot using the data you collect.

5. What is the length of the longest pencil?

_____

6. What is the length of the shortest pencil?

_____

7. What is the difference in length between the shortest and longest pencil?

_____

8. What is the most common pencil length?

_____

9. **A-Z Vocabulary** Use these words to complete the sentences.   **longest   line plot   order**

A _____ can help you see the data in _____ .

A line plot makes it easy to see the shortest and _____ objects.

Problem Solving

Model Use the data in the table to complete the line plot. Then use the line plot to solve the problems.

10.

Crayon Lengths in Centimeters			
6	7	5	6
7	5	7	6
7	8	6	5
5	6	7	6
8	8	6	8

Title: _____

What numbers will you use to make your line plot?

⟷

Label: _____

11. **Higher Order Thinking** How many crayons are longer than 5 centimeters? Explain.

_____

_____

_____

_____

12. ✔**Assessment** Measure the length of the blue crayon to the nearest centimeter. Write the length below.

_____

Then record your measurement on the line plot above that you made in Item 10.

Topic 14 | Lesson 2

Name _____

Another Look! 7 students measured the length of the scissors to the nearest centimeter. The results are shown in the table below.

Length of Scissors in Centimeters			
8	7	7	6
7	6	7	7

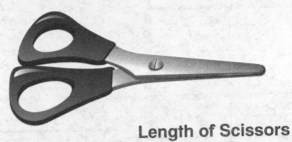

HOME ACTIVITY Have your child measure the lengths of three windows in your home. The windows should have different lengths. Then ask your child to make a line plot of the data.

Step 1 Measure the length of the scissors to the nearest centimeter.

Step 2 Write your measurement in the table above.

Step 3 Record your measurement on the line plot at the right.

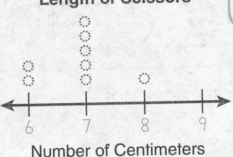

Length of Scissors

Number of Centimeters

Use the line plot above to answer each question.

1. Which measurement of the length of the scissors is most common?

_____ centimeters

2. Why did people get different measurements? Write Yes or No.

_____ The object has a shape that is **NOT** flat.

_____ The measurement is halfway between two units.

_____ The ruler is not aligned with 0 when used.

Model Measure the foot length of 3 friends or family members. Write the measurements in the table below. Then use the data to complete the line plot.

3.

Foot Lengths in Inches			
8	7	8	7
6	9	6	7
10	7	9	10
7			

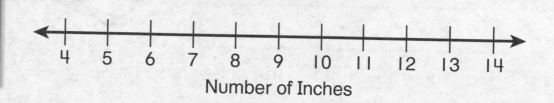

Foot Lengths

4 5 6 7 8 9 10 11 12 13 14

Number of Inches

4. How long is the shortest foot?

5. What is the most common foot length?

6. **Higher Order Thinking** How many people have a foot length that is an even number of inches? Explain.

7. ✓**Assessment** Measure the length of this foot to the nearest inch. Write the length below. Record your measurement on the line plot you made in Item 3.

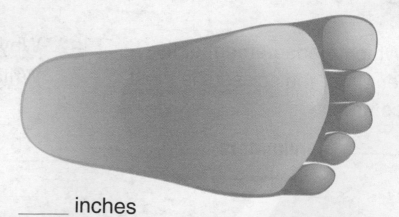

_____ inches

Name _____

Another Look! The table shows how students voted to name the class goldfish.

Use the data from the table to make a bar graph.

HOME ACTIVITY Gather three small groups of objects, such as 3 pens, 4 rubber bands, and 6 buttons. Make a table and a bar graph with your child to show how many of each object you have.

Goldfish Names	
Flash	5
Goldie	3
Rocky	6
Bubbles	8

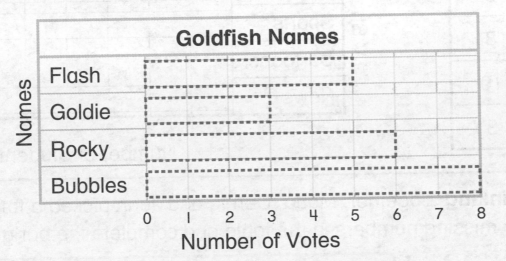

Goldfish Names

Names: Flash, Goldie, Rocky, Bubbles — Number of Votes 0 1 2 3 4 5 6 7 8

Use the bar graph above to solve the problems.

1. How many students voted for the name Goldie or the name Rocky?

   _____

2. How many fewer students voted for the name Flash than voted for the name Rocky?

   _____

3. Which name did the most students vote for? _____

4. Which name did the fewest students vote for? _____

Complete the bar graphs and solve the problems.

5. Model Use the data in the table to complete the bar graph.

Favorite TV Shows	
Animals	6
Sports	8
Cartoons	10
News	3

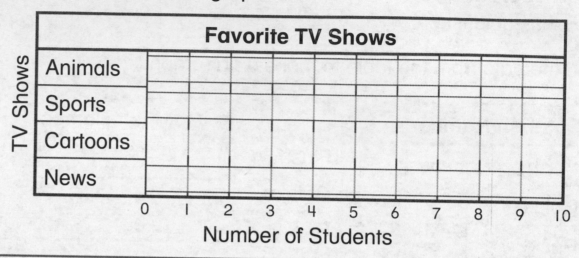

6. Higher Order Thinking Together, Marla, Derek, and Juan picked a total of 19 apples. Write the possible missing numbers in the table and complete the bar graph.

Apple Picking	
Marla	3
Derek	
Juan	

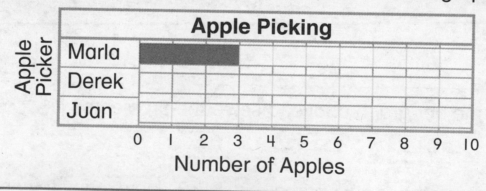

7. ✓**Assessment** Look at the bar graph in Item 5. Which statements are correct? Choose all that apply.

☐ 2 fewer students chose sports than animals.

☐ 5 more students chose sports than news.

☐ 10 students chose news or animals.

☐ 27 students in all were counted.

Name _____

Another Look! A picture graph uses pictures or symbols to show information.

The number at the right tells how many students chose each snack. Complete the picture graph.

There are 9 symbols for popcorn. So 9 students chose popcorn.

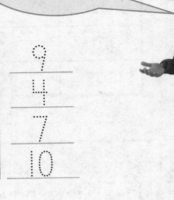

HOME ACTIVITY Tell your child which snack shown in the picture graph is your favorite. Ask him or her to explain how the Favorite Snacks picture graph would change if your response was added to the picture graph.

Favorite Snacks		
Popcorn	☺☺☺☺☺☺☺☺☺	9
Fruit Cup	☺☺☺☺	4
Yogurt	☺☺☺☺☺☺☺	7
Cheese and Crackers	☺☺☺☺☺☺☺☺☺☺	10

Each ☺ = I student

Use the picture graph above to solve the problems.

1. How many students like cheese and crackers best?

_____

2. How many students like yogurt best?

_____

3. Which snack is the least favorite?

_____

4. Which snack is most students' favorite?

_____

Solve each problem.

5. **Model** The tally chart shows how many tickets each student has.
Use the tally chart to complete the picture graph.

Tickets We Have	
Denise	IIII
Steve	II
Tom	⑂⑂ IIII
Lisa	⑂⑂ I

Tickets We Have	
Denise	
Steve	
Tom	
Lisa	

Each 🎫 = I ticket

6. **Higher Order Thinking** Lisa gives 2 tickets to Steve. How many tickets does Steve have now? Explain.

_____

_____

_____

7. ✅**Assessment** The tally chart shows the favorite pets of a class of second graders. Use the tally chart to draw a picture graph.

Favorite Pets	
Cat	⑂⑂ I
Dog	⑂⑂ II
Fish	⑂⑂
Hamster	II

♥ = I Vote

Name _____

Solve & Share

7 students voted for Turtle as their favorite pond animal. 10 students voted for Frog. 4 students voted for Fish. Make a picture graph to show the data. Write two things you notice about the data.

Favorite Pond Animals

Turtle	
Frog	
Fish	

Each ★ = I vote

1. _____

2. _____

Topic 14 | Lesson 5
Digital Resources at SavvasRealize.com
eight hundred twenty-seven **827**

Look at the bar graph. What does it show?

The length of each bar shows how many tickets each person sold.

Leah has sold 2 tickets. Who has sold the most tickets?

Carnival Tickets Sold

Name: Leah, Tino, Kim, Neil

Number of Tickets Sold

You can also compare information and solve problems.

Kim sold the most tickets.

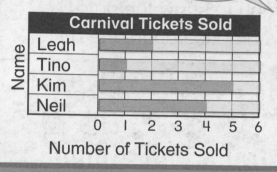

$5 - 1 = 4$ Kim sold 4 more tickets than Tino.

$5 - 4 = 1$ Neil sold 1 less ticket than Kim.

Carnival Tickets Sold

Name: Leah, Tino, Kim, Neil

Number of Tickets Sold

Do You Understand?

Show Me! Look at the graph above. How many tickets did Kim and Neil sell in all? How do you know?

☆ Guided Practice ☆ Use the bar graph to solve the problems.

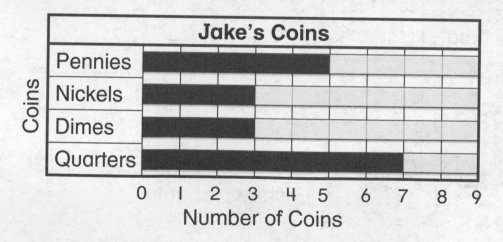

Jake's Coins

Coins: Pennies, Nickels, Dimes, Quarters

Number of Coins

1. How many pennies does Jake have?

5

2. Jake spends 3 of his quarters. How many does he have left?

_____

Tools Assessment

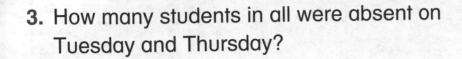 **Independent Practice** ☆ Use the bar graph to solve the problems.

3. How many students in all were absent on Tuesday and Thursday?

_____

4. Were fewer students absent on Monday or Friday? How many fewer?

_____

5. Three of the students absent on Friday were boys. How many girls were absent on Friday?

_____

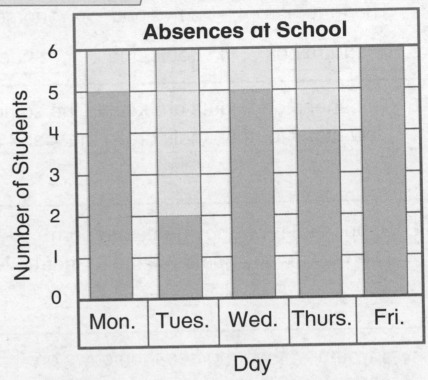

Absences at School

Number of Students

6
5
4
3
2
1
0

Mon. Tues. Wed. Thurs. Fri.

Day

6. On which two days were the same number of students absent?

7. Were more students absent on Wednesday or Thursday? How many more?

8. Higher Order Thinking The graph shows the number of students absent last week. This week, 19 students were absent. Compare the number of students absent this week to the number of students absent last week.

9. **Make Sense** Complete each sentence.

The farm has _____ cows and _____ horses.

The farm has _____ goats and _____ sheep.

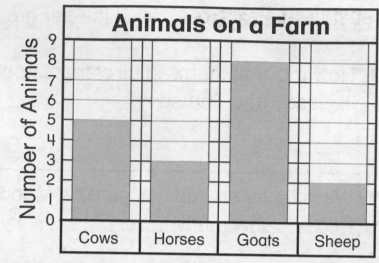

Animals on a Farm

Number of Animals — Type of Animal

10. The sheep and goats are kept in the same pen. How many farm animals are in that pen?

_____

11. Suppose 3 new baby goats are born. Then how many goats will the farmer have?

_____

12. How many fewer horses than cows are on the farm?

_____

13. Write the order of animals on the farm from the greatest number to the least number.

_____

14. **Higher Order Thinking** Do you think the bars on a bar graph should all be the same color? Explain.

_____

15. ✅**Assessment** The farmer wants to buy some sheep. He wants to have as many sheep as cows. How many more sheep should the farmer buy?

_____

Another Look! You can draw conclusions from data in a graph.

This picture graph shows students' favorite types of books.
Write how many students chose each type of book.

The key shows that each book is 1 student's vote. Use the key to count the number of votes.

HOME ACTIVITY Use the Favorite Type of Book picture graph to ask your child questions about the data. Encourage your child to explain each answer.

7
5
4
9

Favorite Type of Book	
Biography	📕📕📕📕📕📕📕
Adventure	📕📕📕📕📕
Science	📕📕📕📕
Mystery	📕📕📕📕📕📕📕📕📕

Each 📕 = 1 vote

Use the picture graph above to answer the questions.

1. Which was the least favorite type of book?

_____

2. Which type of book did most students vote for? _____

3. How many more students voted for biography than for adventure?

4. If each student voted one time only, how many students voted in all?

Use the bar graph to solve each problem.

5. **Make Sense** Complete each sentence.

The fruit basket has ____ apples and ____ pears.

The fruit basket has ____ oranges and ____ plums.

Fruit in a Basket

Pieces of Fruit

8
7
6
5
4
3
2
1
0

Apples | Pears | Oranges | Plums

Type of Fruit

6. Write the order of the type of fruit from the least number to the greatest number.

7. How many apples and oranges in all are in the basket?

8. Maria uses 4 of the pears to make a pie. How many pears are left in the basket?

9. **Higher Order Thinking** Does it matter how you order the data in a bar graph? Explain.

10. ✓**Assessment** How many fewer apples than plums are in the basket?

Name _____

Solve & Share

Make a picture graph to show how many connecting cubes, counters, and ones cubes you have. Then write and solve a problem about your data.

I can ...
reason about data in bar graphs and picture graphs to write and solve problems.

I can also add and subtract using data.

Math Tools	
Connecting Cubes	
Counters	
Ones Cubes	

Each 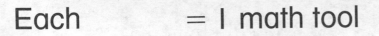 = 1 math tool

_____

_____

_____

The bar graph shows the number of stamps each student has collected.

Write and solve a problem about the data in the bar graph.

Stamp Collections

Student: Ben, Lara, David, Gail

Number of Stamps: 0 1 2 3 4 5 6 7 8 9 10 11 12 13 14 15 16 17 18 19 20 21 22 23 24 25

How can I use reasoning to write and solve a problem?

I can look at the bars to see how many stamps each student has.

I can write a problem to compare the number of stamps two students have.

My Problem

How many more stamps does Lara have than Gail?

25 - 15 = 10
10 more stamps

Do You Understand?

Show Me! Use reasoning to write your own problem about the data in the graph. Then solve it.

☆ **Guided Practice** ☆ Use the bar graph to write and solve problems.

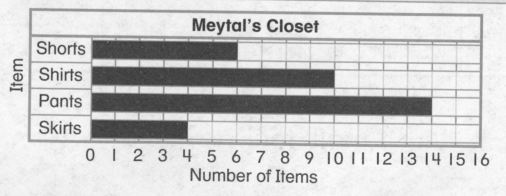

Meytal's Closet

Item: Shorts, Shirts, Pants, Skirts

Number of Items: 0 1 2 3 4 5 6 7 8 9 10 11 12 13 14 15 16

1. How many shirts and skirts are there in all?

$10 \oplus 4 = 14$

2. _____
_____
_____
___ ◯ ___ = ___

Independent Practice

Use the bar graph to write and solve problems.

3. _____

_____

_____

___ ◯ ___ = ___

_____

_____

4. _____

_____

___ ◯ ___ = ___

_____

_____

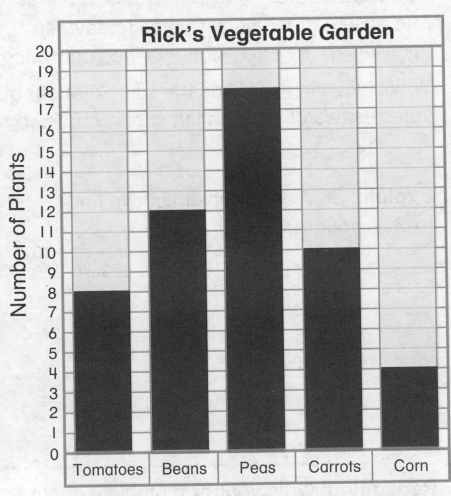

Rick's Vegetable Garden

Number of Plants

Plants: Tomatoes, Beans, Peas, Carrots, Corn

Use reasoning to think about how the numbers, bars, and plants are related.

Problem Solving

Vacation Time!

The picture graph shows votes for favorite vacation spots. Each student voted only once.

Which vacation spot has the same number of votes as two other vacation spots combined?

Votes for Favorite Vacation Spot	
Beach	✓✓✓✓✓✓✓✓✓✓
Mountains	✓✓✓✓✓✓
City	✓✓✓
Theme Park	✓✓✓✓✓✓✓✓✓✓✓✓

Each ✓ = I vote

5. **Explain** Solve the problem above and explain your reasoning.

_____

_____

_____

_____

6. **Make Sense** How many students voted in all? Tell how you know.

_____

_____

_____

_____

7. **Reasoning** Write your own problem about the data in the graph. Then solve it.

_____

_____

_____ ◯ _____ = _____

_____

_____

Another Look! You can reason about data in the picture graph to write and solve problems.

How many more votes did the Tigers get than the Lions?

Votes for Team Name	
Wolves	
Tigers	
Lions	

Each = 1 vote

HOME ACTIVITY Look at the picture graph for team names together. Ask your child to find how many more votes there are for Wolves and Lions combined than there are for Tigers. Have your child explain how to find the answer.

Count the symbols for the votes for Tigers and Lions on the picture graph. Then subtract.

Tigers 10   Lions 8

10 – 8 = 2

The Tigers got 2 more votes than the Lions.

Write and solve problems about the data in the picture graph above.

1. _____

___ ◯ ___ = ___

2. _____

___ ◯ ___ = ___

Gym Games

Ms. Winn has to cut one game from gym class. So, she asked students to choose their favorite game. The bar graph shows the results. Each student voted only once. Which game should she cut and why?

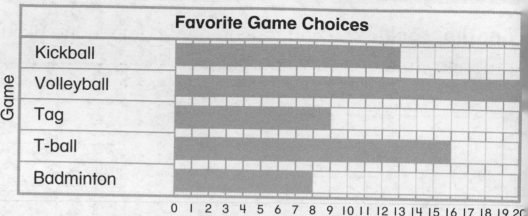

Favorite Game Choices

Game: Kickball, Volleyball, Tag, T-ball, Badminton

0 1 2 3 4 5 6 7 8 9 10 11 12 13 14 15 16 17 18 19 20
Number of Students

3. **Make Sense** How many students voted for each game? Tell how you know.

_____

_____

_____

_____

4. **Explain** Ms. Winn wants to cut tag from gym class. Do you agree? Explain.

_____

_____

_____

_____

5. **Reasoning** How many fewer students chose tag and badminton combined than volleyball? Explain your reasoning.

_____

_____

_____

_____

Find a partner. Point to a clue. Read the clue.

Look below the clues to find a match. Write the clue letter in the box next to the match.

Find a match for every clue.

I can …
add and subtract within 100.

Clues

A The difference is less than 16.

B The sum equals 43 + 25.

C The difference equals 75 − 46.

D The sum equals 53 + 20.

E The difference equals 96 − 19.

F The sum equals 75.

G The sum is between 60 and 65.

H The difference is between 25 and 28.

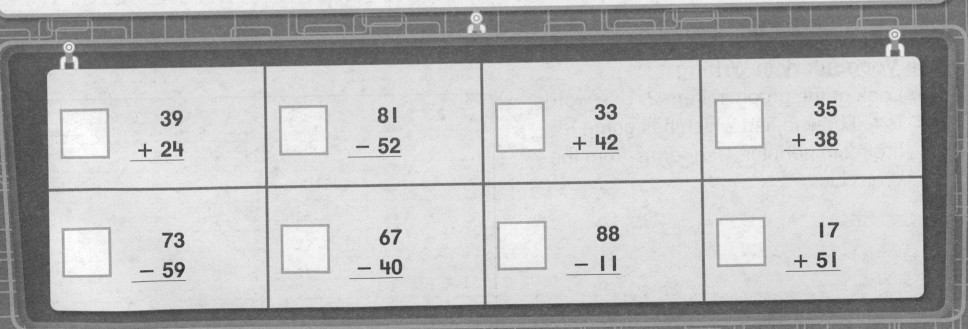

| □ 39 + 24 | □ 81 − 52 | □ 33 + 42 | □ 35 + 38 |
| □ 73 − 59 | □ 67 − 40 | □ 88 − 11 | □ 17 + 51 |

Word List
- bar graph
- data
- line plot
- picture graph
- symbol

Understand Vocabulary

Label each data display. Write *line plot*, *bar graph*, or *picture graph*.

1.

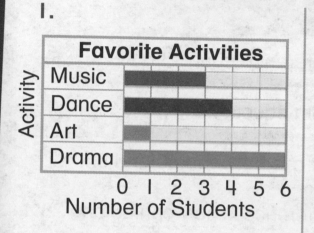

Favorite Activities

Activity	Number of Students
Music	
Dance	
Art	
Drama	

0 1 2 3 4 5 6
Number of Students

_____

2.

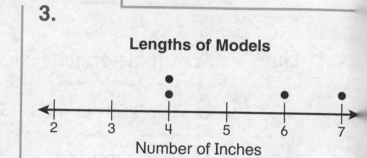

Favorite Ball Games

Baseball	♀♀
Soccer	♀♀♀♀♀♀♀
Tennis	♀♀♀

Each ♀ = 1 student

_____

3.

Lengths of Models

Number of Inches

_____

Use Vocabulary in Writing

4. Look at the graph in Item 2. Use words to tell how to find which ball game is the most popular. Use terms from the Word List.

_____
_____
_____
_____
_____

Set A

Line plots show and organize data.
Use an inch ruler. Measure the length of
the toy car. Then record the measurement
in the table.

Complete the table and show
the data on a line plot.

1. Use an inch ruler. Measure the length of
the pencil. Then record the measurement
in the table.

Toy	Length in Inches
Car	3
Airplane	5
Doll	5
Block	1

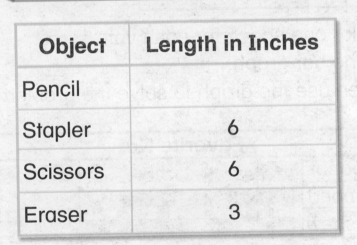

Object	Length in Inches
Pencil	
Stapler	6
Scissors	6
Eraser	3

Place a dot over the number that shows
the length of each toy.

Length of Toys

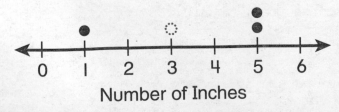

Number of Inches

2. Make a line plot to show each length.

Length of Objects

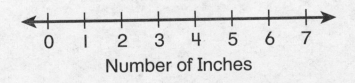

Number of Inches

You can make a bar graph to show the data in a table.

Students voted for their favorite nut. The table shows the number of votes.

Favorite Nut	
Peanut	7
Almond	4
Cashew	5

Color one space for each vote in the bar graph.

Then use the graph to solve the problem.

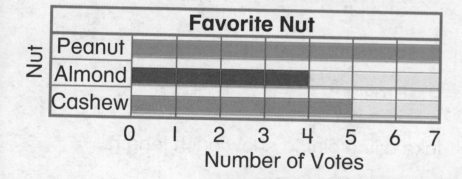

Favorite Nut

How many students voted? ___16___

Use the table to complete the bar graph. Then solve each problem.

3.

Favorite Yogurt	
Lemon	3
Vanilla	7
Banana	6

Favorite Yogurt

Flavor — Lemon, Vanilla, Banana

0 1 2 3 4 5 6 7

Number of Votes

4. How many more students voted for vanilla than banana? _____

5. How many fewer students voted for lemon than vanilla? _____

Name _____

Set C

A picture graph uses pictures or symbols to show data.

The tally chart shows votes for favorite sea animals.

Favorite Sea Animals	
Whale	THH I
Dolphin	II
Seal	IIII

Use the data to make a picture graph.
Each ⚲ stands for I vote.

Favorite Sea Animals	
Whale	⚲⚲⚲⚲⚲⚲
Dolphin	⚲⚲
Seal	⚲⚲⚲⚲

⚲ = I vote

Which sea animal has the fewest votes?

dolphin

Use the tally chart to complete the picture graph.
Then solve each problem.

6.

Favorite Birds	
Blue Jay	THH
Robin	THH III
Seagull	THH THH

Favorite Birds	
Blue Jay	
Robin	
Seagull	

🐦 = I vote

7. How many votes did seagull get?

_____

8. Which bird had the fewest votes?

_____

eight hundred forty-three **843**

Thinking Habits

Reasoning

What do the symbols mean?

How are the numbers in the problem related?

How can I write a word problem using the information that is given?

How do the numbers in my problem relate to each other?

How can I use a word problem to show what an equation means?

Use the picture graph to solve each problem. Each student voted once.

Favorite Winter Sport	
Skiing	❄❄❄❄❄❄❄
Snowboarding	❄❄❄❄❄❄❄❄❄
Skating	❄❄❄❄❄❄❄❄
Ice Fishing	❄❄❄❄

Each ❄ = I vote

9. How many fewer students chose ice fishing than snowboarding? _____

10. Write and solve your own problem about the data.

_____

_____

___ ◯ ___ = ___

1. Pam has 5 pennies, 2 nickels, 8 dimes, and 9 quarters. Show this data in the bar graph below. Draw the bars.

Pam's Coin Collection

Coin

| Pennies |
| Nickels |
| Dimes |
| Quarters |

0 1 2 3 4 5 6 7 8 9 10

Number of Coins

2. Use the bar graph you made above. Pam spends 5 of her dimes to buy an apple. Now how many dimes does Pam have left?

Ⓐ 13

Ⓑ 5

Ⓒ 3

Ⓓ 0

3. Is each sentence about the picture graph correct? Choose Yes or No.

Favorite Camp Activity

Crafts	𝓍 𝓍 𝓍
Swimming	𝓍 𝓍 𝓍 𝓍 𝓍
Archery	𝓍 𝓍
Tennis	𝓍 𝓍 𝓍 𝓍 𝓍 𝓍

Each 𝓍 = 1 camper

7 students voted for tennis. ◯ Yes ◯ No

16 students voted in all. ◯ Yes ◯ No

2 more students voted for swimming than for crafts. ◯ Yes ◯ No

3 fewer students voted for tennis than for crafts. ◯ Yes ◯ No

4. How many more tickets did Kendra sell than Leon?

Ⓐ 5

Ⓑ 6

Ⓒ 11

Ⓓ 17

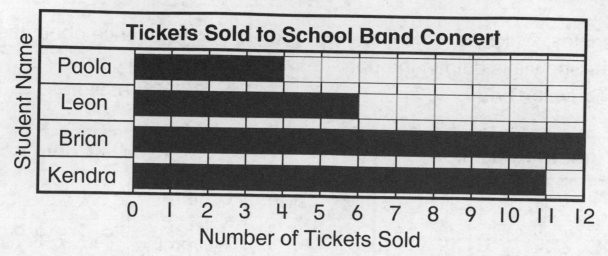

Tickets Sold to School Band Concert

Student Name: Paola, Leon, Brian, Kendra

Number of Tickets Sold

5. Complete the table and the line plot.

Part A

Use a centimeter ruler. Measure the length of the crayon to the nearest centimeter. Write the length in the table below.

Crayon Lengths in Centimeters			
5	7	7	8
4	7	5	

Part B

Use the data in the table to complete the line plot.

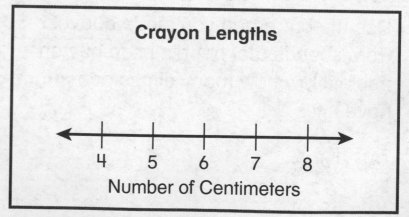

Crayon Lengths

4   5   6   7   8

Number of Centimeters

What is the difference in length between the shortest and longest crayon?

_____

6. Scott is making a picture graph from the data in the tally chart.
How many symbols should he draw in the bottom row?

Favorite Fruit	
Apple	IIII
Banana	卌 I
Pear	I
Orange	卌

Favorite Fruit	
Apple	🙂 🙂 🙂 🙂
Banana	🙂 🙂 🙂 🙂 🙂 🙂
Pear	🙂
Orange	

Each 🙂 = I student

Ⓐ 3   Ⓑ 4   Ⓒ 5   Ⓓ 6

---

7. Mary gets new stamps every month.
The bar graph shows the number of stamps she collects each month.

Which statements are true? Choose all that apply.

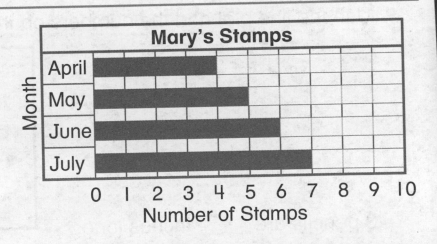

☐ Mary collects I more stamp in May than she does in April.

☐ Mary collects 2 fewer stamps in June than she does in July.

☐ Mary collects a total of II stamps in May and June.

☐ Mary collects one additional stamp each month from May to July.

8. Use the tally chart to complete the picture graph.
Then use the picture graph to solve the problems.

Favorite Flower	
Rose	ⵜⵜⵜ I
Daisy	III
Tulip	ⵜⵜⵜ
Lily	ⵜⵜⵜ III

Favorite Flower	
Rose	
Daisy	
Tulip	
Lily	

Each = I vote

How many students voted for Lily? _____

Which flower is the least favorite? _____

9. Use the line plot and the numbers on the cards to complete each sentence.

 3   4   5   7

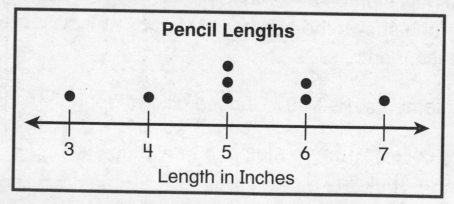

3 pencils are _____ inches long.

The longest pencil is _____ inches long.

The shortest pencil is _____ inches long.

The difference between the shortest and longest pencil is _____ inches.

Name _____

School Surveys

Some students asked their classmates different questions.

George asked his classmates to vote on their favorite lunch. This table shows the results.

Favorite Lunch	
Taco	5
Pizza	8
Hamburger	9
Salad	6

1. Use the table to complete the bar graph.

Favorite Lunch

Lunch									
Taco									
Pizza									
Hamburger									
Salad									

 1 2 3 4 5 6 7 8 9
Number of Students

2. Use the Favorite Lunch table to complete the picture graph.

Favorite Lunch	
Taco	
Pizza	
Hamburger	
Salad	

Each ✔ = 1 student

3. Use the graphs you made to answer these questions.

How many students chose salad as their favorite lunch? _____

Which lunch is the favorite of the most students? _____

How would the bar graph change if two more students chose Taco?

_____

_____

4. Write and solve a math story about the Favorite Lunch graphs you made.

Part A

Use the bar graph or the picture graph about favorite lunches to write a math story problem. The problem should include addition or subtraction.

_____

_____

_____

Part B

Solve your math story problem. Explain how you solved the problem.

_____

_____

_____

_____

5. Gina asked her classmates to measure the length of their favorite storybook in inches. She recorded their measurements in this table.

Lengths of Books in Inches			
12	9	8	10
6	10	11	9
10	9	9	12
12	10	7	7

Part A

Use the table to make a line plot.

Part B

What is the difference in length between the longest and shortest books?

_____ inches

Shapes and Their Attributes

Essential Question: How can shapes be described, compared, and broken into parts?

Digital Resources

Solve Learn Glossary

Tools Assessment Help Games

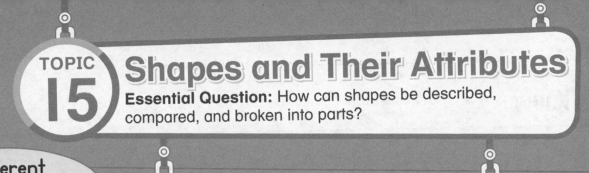

Different tools have different shapes!

How does the shape of a tool help it work?

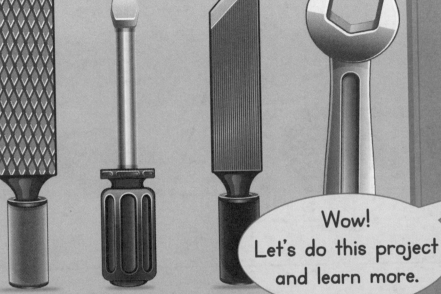

Wow! Let's do this project and learn more.

Math and Science Project: All About Shape

Find Out Draw pictures of tools used for gardening, cooking, or fixing. Describe the shape of each tool. Tell how the shape of each tool helps it work.

Journal: Make a Book Show your work in a book. In your book, also:

- Choose a tool that you use at school. Tell how the shape of the tool helps it work.

- Draw and describe polygon shapes.

Name _____

Review What You Know

A-Z Vocabulary

1. Circle the shape that has 6 **sides**.

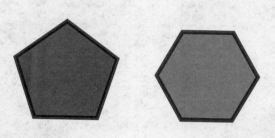

2. Circle each **plane shape**. Put a box around each **solid figure**.

3. Put a box around the circle that shows **fourths**.

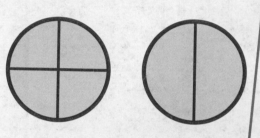

Basic Facts

4. Write each sum.

$$\begin{array}{r} 5 \\ +8 \\ \hline \end{array} \qquad \begin{array}{r} 7 \\ +7 \\ \hline \end{array} \qquad \begin{array}{r} 10 \\ +10 \\ \hline \end{array}$$

5. Write each difference.

$$\begin{array}{r} 17 \\ -9 \\ \hline \end{array} \qquad \begin{array}{r} 15 \\ -6 \\ \hline \end{array} \qquad \begin{array}{r} 12 \\ -8 \\ \hline \end{array}$$

Rectangles

6. Find the distance around.

10 ft

7 ft

_____

My Word Cards

Study the words on the front of the card.
Complete the activity on the back.

vertices (vertex)

quadrilateral

pentagon

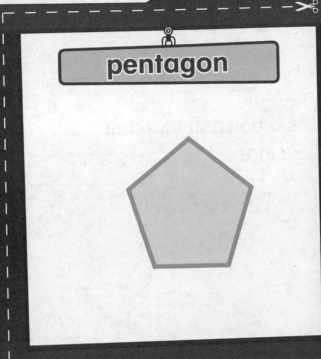

hexagon

polygon

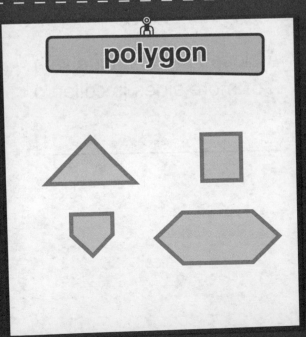

angle

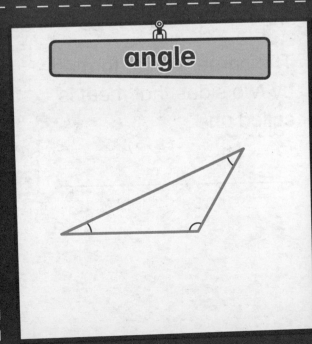

Use what you know to complete the sentences.
Extend learning by writing your own sentence using each word.

A _____

is a polygon that has
5 sides.

A _____

is a polygon that has
4 sides.

_____

are corner points where
2 sides of a polygon meet
or where edges of a solid
figure meet.

One corner point is called a

_____.

The corner shape formed
by two sides that meet is
called an

_____.

A closed plane shape with
3 or more sides is called a

_____.

A _____

is a polygon that has
6 sides.

My Word Cards

Study the words on the front of the card.
Complete the activity on the back.

A-Z
Glossary

right angle

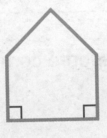

cube

face

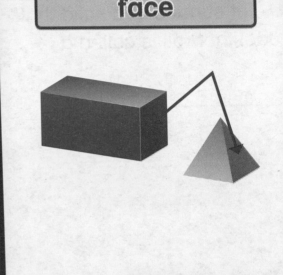

edge

equal shares

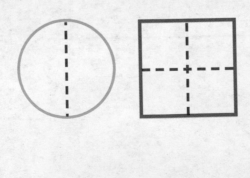

halves

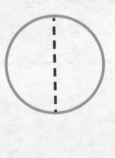

My Word Cards

Use what you know to complete the sentences.
Extend learning by writing your own sentence using each word.

A flat surface of a solid that does not roll is called a

_____.

A _____

is a solid figure with six faces that are matching squares.

A _____

_____

forms a square corner.

When a whole is divided into 2 equal shares, the shares are called

_____.

Parts of a whole that are the same size are called

_____.

A line formed where two faces of a solid figure meet is called an

_____.

My Word Cards

Study the words on the front of the card.
Complete the activity on the back.

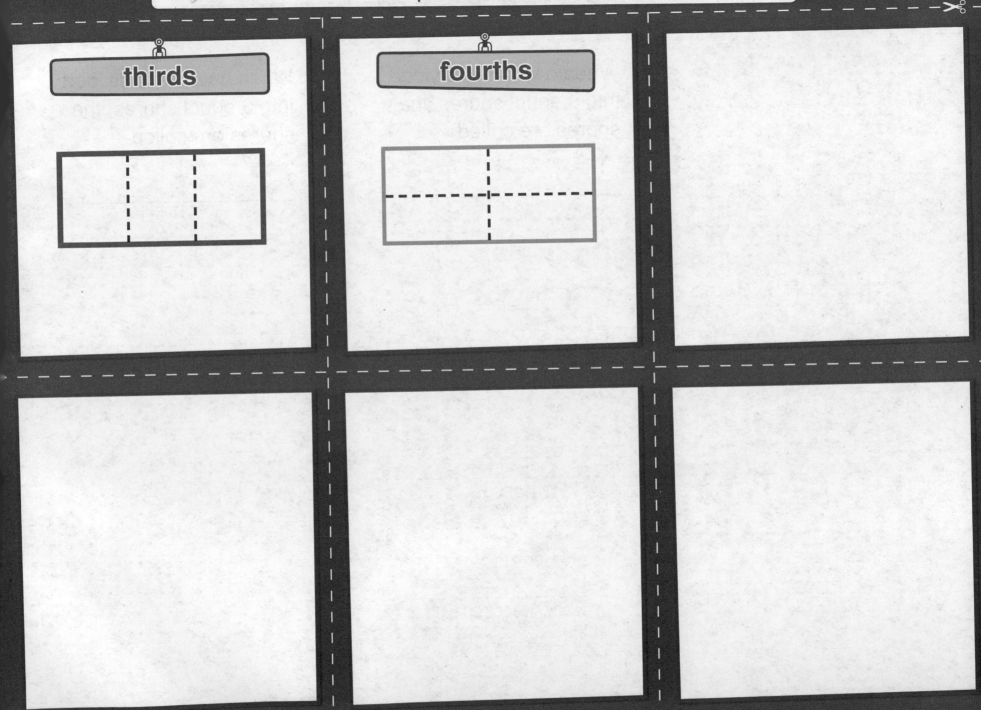

thirds

fourths

My Word Cards

When a whole is divided into 4 equal shares, the shares are called

_____.

When a whole is divided into 3 equal shares, the shares are called

_____.

⭐ ndependent Practice ⭐ Match each shape to its name.

4.

5.

triangle quadrilateral pentagon hexagon

triangle quadrilateral pentagon hexagon

Draw the shape. Tell how many sides and vertices.

6. Quadrilateral

_____ sides

_____ vertices

7. Hexagon

_____ sides

_____ vertices

8. Triangle

_____ sides

_____ vertices

9. Higher Order Thinking Bianca drew a triangle and a pentagon.
How many sides and vertices did she draw in all? Draw the shapes.

_____ sides   _____ vertices

10. **Model** Marcos has
4 toothpicks.
He places them as shown.
What shape can Marcos
make if he adds one more
toothpick?

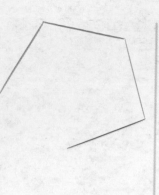

_____

11. (A-Z) **Vocabulary** Connect all the dots to
make two shapes that have **vertices.**
Name the shapes that you make.

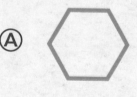

_____   _____

12. **Higher Order Thinking** Randall said that
a square is a quadrilateral.
Susan said that a square is a square, so
it is not a quadrilateral. Who is correct?
Explain.

_____

_____

_____

_____

13. ✓**Assessment** Which polygon is
NOT a hexagon?

Ⓐ

Ⓑ

Ⓒ

Ⓓ

Think: What
do I know about
hexagons?

Topic 15 | Lesson 1

Name _____

 Help Tools Games

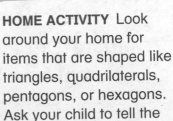

Homework & Practice 15-1

2-Dimensional Shapes

Another Look! You can name shapes by their number of sides and vertices.

 A triangle has
3 sides and
3 vertices.

 A quadrilateral has
4 sides and
4 vertices.

 A pentagon has
5 sides and
5 vertices.

 A hexagon has
6 sides and
6 vertices.

HOME ACTIVITY Look around your home for items that are shaped like triangles, quadrilaterals, pentagons, or hexagons. Ask your child to tell the number of sides and vertices for each shape.

Name each shape.
Write the number of sides and vertices.

1.

Shape: _____

____ sides

____ vertices

2.

Shape: _____

____ sides

____ vertices

3.

Shape: _____

____ sides

____ vertices

Topic 15 | Lesson 1

Digital Resources at SavvasRealize.com

eight hundred sixty-three **863**

Tell how many sides or vertices each student drew.

4. **Algebra** Leona drew 2 pentagons.

She drew _____ vertices.

5. **Algebra** Nestor drew 3 quadrilaterals.

He drew _____ sides.

6. **Algebra** Kip drew a hexagon and a triangle.

He drew _____ vertices.

7. **Model** Draw 2 hexagons that look different from the one shown.

8. **Model** Draw 2 quadrilaterals that look different from the one shown.

9. **Higher Order Thinking** Tami traced the flat sides of this wooden block. What shapes did she draw? Name and draw the shapes.

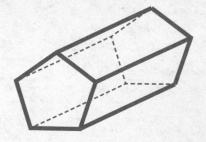

10. ✅ **Assessment** Jin drew two polygons. One of the polygons is shown below. If Jin drew 9 sides and 9 vertices in all, which other polygon did he draw?

Ⓐ triangle

Ⓒ rectangle

Ⓑ rhombus

Ⓓ pentagon

Independent Practice ☆ Write the number of angles and then name the shape.

5.  _____ angles

Shape: _____

6. _____ angles

Shape: _____

7.  _____ angles

Shape: _____

8. _____ angles

Shape: _____

9. _____ angles

Shape: _____

10. _____ angles

Shape: _____

11. Higher Order Thinking Draw a polygon with 2 right angles and 2 angles that are not right angles. Name the shape you draw.

How many angles will your polygon have in all?

12. **Be Precise** Which plane shapes are sewn together in the soccer ball?

_____

_____

13. **Math and Science** Bees make honeycomb. The honeycomb shape uses the least amount of wax. Name the shape. Tell how many angles the shape has.

14. **Higher Order Thinking** Draw a polygon shape that has 7 angles.
How many sides does the polygon have?
How many vertices does it have?

15. ✓**Assessment** Name the shape of the sign below. Write 3 things that describe the shape.

_____

_____

_____

Name _____

Another Look! Polygons are closed plane shapes with 3 or more sides. Polygons have the same number of angles and vertices as sides.

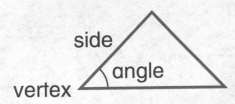

side

angle

vertex

An angle that forms a square corner is called a right angle.

HOME ACTIVITY Ask your child to find objects that have polygon shapes. Have your child name each shape and tell how many angles it has.

Name and describe this polygon.

Pentagon 5 sides 5 vertices 5 angles

Write the number of angles and then name the shape.

1.

_____ angles

Shape: _____

2.

_____ angles

Shape: _____

3.

_____ angles

Shape: _____

Topic 15 | Lesson 2

Digital Resources at SavvasRealize.com

eight hundred sixty-nine **869**

Solve each problem.

4. Be Precise The sign below tells drivers to yield. This means to wait for other cars or people to go first.
Which polygon shape do you see in the sign?

5. 🔤 **Vocabulary** The outside edges of this nut for a bolt form a **polygon** shape. Name that shape.

6. Higher Order Thinking Look at the design below. Write three names for the shape that has right angles.

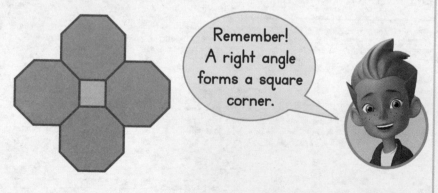

Remember! A right angle forms a square corner.

7. ✅ **Assessment** Name the shape below. Write 3 things that describe the shape.

Independent Practice   Draw each shape. Complete the sentences.

3. Draw a polygon with
3 vertices and
1 right angle.

The polygon also has

_____ sides.

The polygon is

a _____ .

4. Draw a quadrilateral with
opposite sides that are
the same length.

The polygon also has

_____ vertices.

The polygon is

a _____ .

5. Draw a polygon with
4 sides that are
the same length.

The polygon also has

_____ angles.

The polygon is

a _____ .

---

6. Draw a polygon with
4 sides that are
different lengths.

The polygon also has

_____ angles.

The polygon is

a _____ .

7. Draw a polygon with
5 vertices and 3 sides
that are the same length.

The polygon also has

_____ sides in all.

The polygon is

a _____ .

8. Higher Order Thinking
Can you draw a polygon
with 3 vertices and
4 sides? Explain.

9. Be Precise Draw a rectangle with 4 equal sides.

What is another name for this shape?

_____

10. Draw 3 shapes. The first shape is a quadrilateral. The number of vertices in each shape increases by one.

Name the third shape. _____

11. Higher Order Thinking The owner of Joe's Fish Market wants a new sign. He wants the sign to have curved sides. Draw a sign for Joe's Fish Market.

Is the sign a polygon? Explain.

_____

_____

12. ✅ **Assessment** David drew two different polygons. One of the polygons was a square. If David drew 9 sides and 9 vertices in all, what other polygon did David draw?

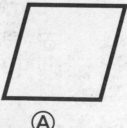
Ⓐ

Ⓒ

Ⓑ

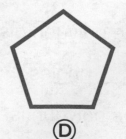
Ⓓ

Name _____

Another Look! The number of sides in a polygon is the same as the number of vertices and the number of angles.

Draw a polygon with 6 vertices.

The sides can be the same length.   The sides can be different lengths.

HOME ACTIVITY Ask your child to draw a polygon with 4 vertices. Then ask your child to tell you the name of the polygon and how many sides and angles it has.

Each polygon has __6__ vertices.

Each polygon also has __6__ sides and __6__ angles.

Both polygons are _hexagons_ .

What pattern do you see?

Draw two different polygons for each number of vertices.

1. 4 vertices

2. 5 vertices

Each polygon has _____ sides.

Both polygons are _____ .

Each polygon has _____ angles.

Both polygons are _____ .

Draw each polygon. Then complete the sentences.

3. It has 2 fewer sides than a pentagon.

The shape is a _____.

4. It has 3 more vertices than a triangle.

The shape is a _____.

5. **Make Sense** It has 1 less vertex than a hexagon and 2 more angles than a triangle.

The shape is a _____.

6. **Higher Order Thinking** Tanika has 7 toothpicks. She uses them all to create two polygons. Draw two polygons that Tanika could have created. Write the names of your shapes.

7. ✅**Assessment** Kit drew a polygon that has 4 vertices. Which could **NOT** be Kit's polygon?

quadrilateral
Ⓐ

rectangle
Ⓒ

triangle
Ⓑ

square
Ⓓ

8. ✅**Assessment** Reg drew a polygon with more sides than a square and fewer vertices than a hexagon. Which could Reg have drawn?

triangle
Ⓐ

quadrilateral
Ⓒ

rectangle
Ⓑ

pentagon
Ⓓ

Independent Practice

Decide if the shape is a cube. Then draw a line from each shape to *cube* or **NOT** a cube.

3.

cube

NOT a cube

4. Trace the cube shown below.

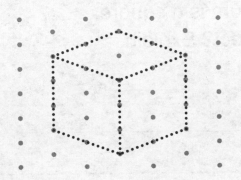

How many faces can you see?

_____ faces

Algebra Use what you know about cubes to write an equation and solve each problem.

5. How many vertices do these two cubes have in all?

_____ + _____ = _____

_____ vertices

6. How many faces do these two cubes have in all?

_____ + _____ = _____

_____ faces

7. **Explain** Scott is holding a solid figure with 6 equal faces, 12 edges, and 8 vertices. Scott says the figure is a cube. Carmen says the figure is a square.
Who is correct? Explain.

_____

_____

_____

8. **Vocabulary** Circle the vocabulary word that completes the sentence.

vertices　　　**faces**　　　**edges**

A cube has 6 _____.

9. **Higher Order Thinking** Use a place-value ones cube or another solid cube.
Look at the cube as you turn it.
Turn the cube in any direction.

What is the greatest number of faces you can see at one time? Explain.

_____

_____

10. **Assessment** Complete the sentences about a cube.

A cube is a solid _____.

A cube has _____ equal faces,

_____ vertices, and _____ edges.

Name _____

Another Look! You can tell if a shape is a cube by counting its faces, vertices, and edges. Number cubes are examples of real-life objects that are cubes.

Every cube has 6 equal square faces, 8 vertices, and 12 edges.

HOME ACTIVITY Have your child find an object at home that has a cube shape. Ask your child to describe the object including the number of faces, vertices, and edges.

These real-life objects are **NOT** cubes.

Tell whether each shape or object is a cube. If it is not a cube, tell what shape it is. Then explain how you know.

1. _____

_____

_____

_____

2. _____

_____

_____

_____

Topic 15 | Lesson 4   Digital Resources at SavvasRealize.com   eight hundred eighty-one **881**

Use what you know about cubes to solve each problem.

3. **Look for Patterns** You can make two squares to draw a cube.

1. Connect the 4 blue dots to make one square.
2. Connect the 4 green dots to make another square.
3. Connect each corner of the blue square to a like corner of the green square.

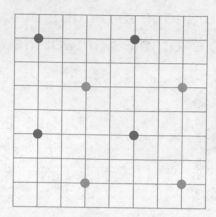

This is another way to draw a cube.

---

4. **Higher Order Thinking** Look at the solid figure below. Count the number of faces, vertices, and edges it has. Why is this figure **NOT** a cube?

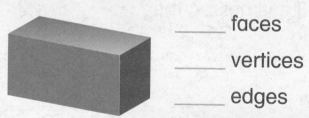

_____ faces

_____ vertices

_____ edges

_____

_____

5. ✅**Assessment** Circle the shapes that are **NOT** cubes. Explain how you know.

_____

Name _____

Solve & Share

How many equal squares cover this rectangle?
How could you show this with an addition equation?

Columns

Rows

_____ equal squares

Equation: _____

Digital Resources at SavvasRealize.com

How many red squares can cover this rectangle?

Begin like this:

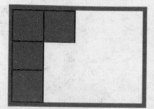

NOT like this:

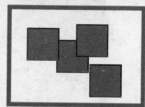

Count. Each row has 4 squares. You can add the squares by rows.

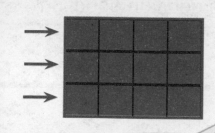

$4 + 4 + 4 = 12$

Count. Each column has 3 squares. You can add the squares by columns.

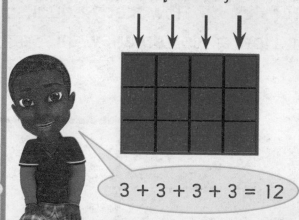

$3 + 3 + 3 + 3 = 12$

Do You Understand?

Show Me! Explain how you can divide a rectangle into equal squares.

☆ Guided Practice   Solve.

1. Use square tiles to cover the rectangle. Trace the tiles. Column 1 is done for you.

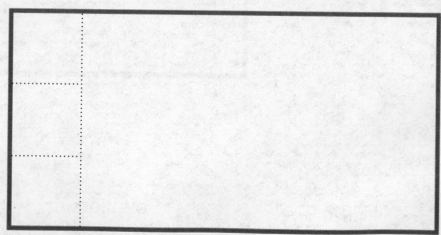

2. Count and add. How many squares cover the rectangle?

Add by rows: ＿＿ + ＿＿ + ＿＿ = ＿＿

Add by columns:

＿＿ + ＿＿ + ＿＿ + ＿＿ + ＿＿ + ＿＿ = ＿＿

Topic 15 | Lesson 5

☆ Independent ☆ Practice

Use square tiles to cover each rectangle. Trace the tiles. Count the squares.

3.

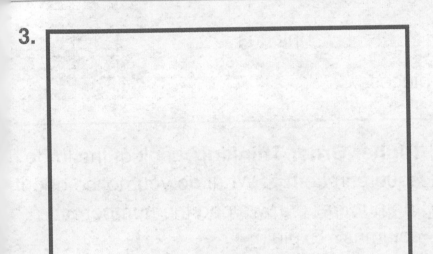

Add by rows:

____ + ____ + ____ + ____ = ____

Add by columns:

____ + ____ + ____ + ____ + ____

= ____

4.

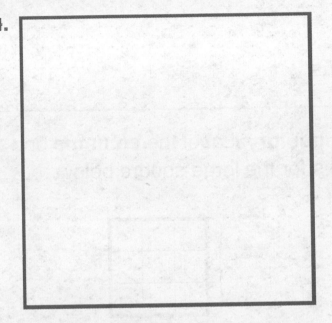

Add by rows:

____ + ____ + ____ + ____ = ____

Add by columns:

____ + ____ + ____ + ____ = ____

---

5. Number Sense Draw a rectangle that is divided into 6 equal squares.

Problem Solving ✶ Solve each problem.

6. Look for Patterns Lisa bakes corn bread. She cuts it into equal square pieces. How many equal squares do you see?
Write two equations to show the total number of square pieces.

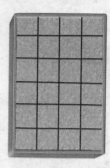

Rows: _____ + _____ + _____ + _____ + _____ + _____ = _____ pieces

Columns: _____ + _____ + _____ + _____ = _____ pieces

---

7. **A-Z Vocabulary** Label the **columns** and the **rows** for the large square below.

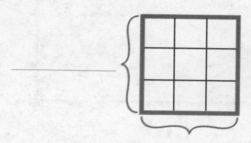

8. Higher Order Thinking Look at the large square in Item 7. What do you notice about the number of rows and the number of columns? Explain.

_____

_____

_____

_____

---

9. ✔**Assessment** Count the equal squares in the rows and columns of the rectangle. Then use the numbers on the cards to write the missing numbers in the equations.

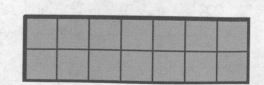

Rows: _____ + _____ = _____

Columns: _____ + _____ + _____ + _____ + _____ + _____ + _____ = _____

Topic 15 | Lesson 5

Name _____

Another Look! How many squares cover this rectangle?

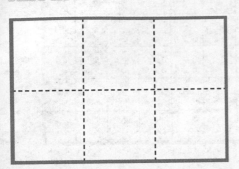

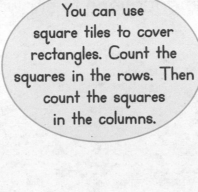

You can use square tiles to cover rectangles. Count the squares in the rows. Then count the squares in the columns.

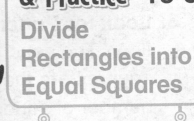

HOME ACTIVITY Ask your child to draw a rectangular section of a floor made of square tiles. Then ask your child to count how many squares make up that rectangle.

Add the rows: $3 + 3 = 6$

Add the columns: $2 + 2 + 2 = 6$

Use square tiles to cover the rectangle. Trace the tiles. Count the squares.

1.

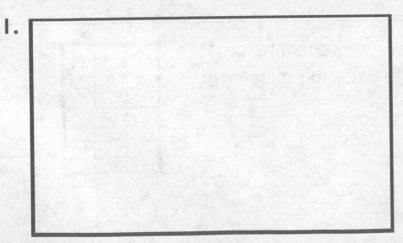

2. How many squares cover the rectangle?

Add by rows:

___ + ___ + ___ = ___

Add by columns:

___ + ___ + ___ + ___ + ___

= ___

Solve each problem.

3. Look for Patterns Mr. Cory puts square tiles on the kitchen floor. The square tiles are all the same size. How many equal squares are there? Write two equations to show the total number of square tiles.

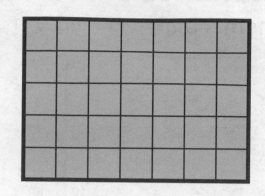

Rows:

____ + ____ + ____ + ____ + ____ = ____ tiles

Columns:

____ + ____ + ____ + ____ + ____ + ____ + ____ = ____ tiles

---

4. Higher Order Thinking 10 friends want to equally share a rectangular pan of granola bars. Show how to divide the rectangle into 10 equal pieces.

---

5. **Assessment** Count the equal squares in the rows and columns of the rectangle. Then use the numbers on the cards to write the missing numbers in the equations.

| 4 | 12 | 3 |

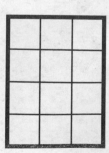

Rows: ____ + ____ + ____ + ____ = ____

Columns: ____ + ____ + ____ = ____

Name _____

Divide each shape into the number of equal shares given. Show 2 ways. Then complete the sentences.

3. 3 equal shares

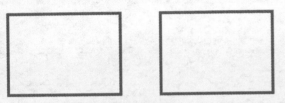

Each share is _____ the whole.

Each whole is _____.

4. 4 equal shares

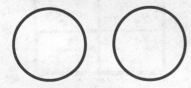

Each share is _____ the whole.

Each whole is _____.

5. 2 equal shares

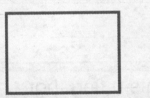 

Each share is _____ the whole.

Each whole is _____.

6. Higher Order Thinking Draw what comes next.

     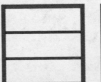

7. Model Leon cut a waffle into halves. Draw lines to show 3 different ways he could have cut the waffle.

8. Math and Science Tina is planting a garden. She wants to have equal parts for beans, for tomatoes, and for peppers. Draw a picture of how she could divide her garden.

9. Higher Order Thinking Draw lines on the picture to solve the problem.

4 friends want to share a watermelon. How could they cut the watermelon so each friend gets an equal share?

Each friend will get _____.

10. ✔Assessment Matt wants a flag that shows fourths. Which flags could Matt use? Choose all that apply.

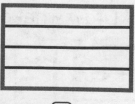

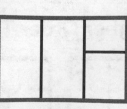

Another Look! Equal shares are the same size.

2 equal shares

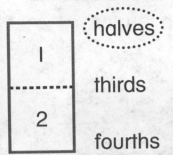

(halves)

thirds

fourths

3 equal shares

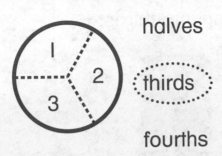

halves

(thirds)

fourths

4 equal shares

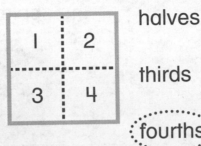

halves

thirds

(fourths)

HOME ACTIVITY Draw three squares. Ask your child to draw lines in one square to show halves. Then have your child draw lines in the second square to show thirds, and draw lines in the third square to show fourths.

Draw the number of equal shares given for each shape. Then circle the word that describes the shares.

1. 4 equal shares

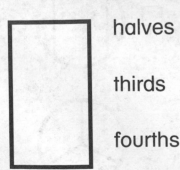

halves

thirds

fourths

2. 3 equal shares

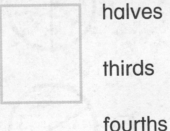

halves

thirds

fourths

3. 2 equal shares

halves

thirds

fourths

4. 4 equal shares

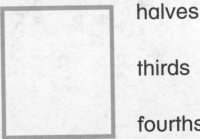

halves

thirds

fourths

5. Two students want to equally share a small pizza. Draw how to split the pizza into halves.

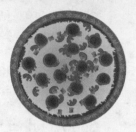

6. Three students want to equally share a tray of apple crisp. Draw two ways to split the apple crisp into thirds.

7. Four students want to share an apple pie. Draw lines to split the pie into fourths.

8. Higher Order Thinking This shape is divided into four pieces. Ryan says this shape is divided into fourths. Is he correct? Explain.

_____

_____

9. ✅**Assessment** Tom cut his muffin in half to share it with his brother. Which pictures do **NOT** show halves? Choose all that apply.

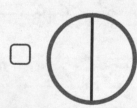 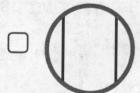

Name _____

Draw lines to show two different ways to divide the same rectangle into 4 equal shares. Then answer the questions.

4. Show equal shares that are the **same shape**.   Show equal shares that are **different shapes**.

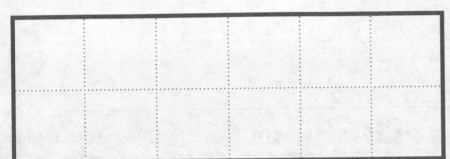
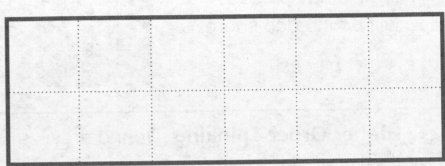

5. How many squares are in each equal share in Item 4? _____

6. Describe the equal shares and the whole in Item 4.

Each share is _____ the whole.

Each whole is _____.

Draw lines to show two different ways to divide the same rectangle into 3 equal shares.

7.
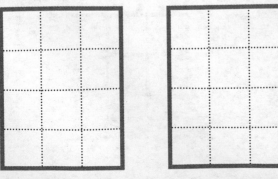

8. Higher Order Thinking How can equal shares in a rectangle have different shapes?

_____

_____

_____

9. Allen wants to share this pan of corn bread with 3 friends. Allen and his friends will each get an equal share.

How many pieces will be in each share?

_____ pieces

10. **Explain** Greg says that equal shares can be different in shape and size. Is Greg correct? Explain.

_____

_____

11. **Higher Order Thinking** Donna drew the line in this rectangle to make 2 equal shares. Are the shares equal? Why or why not?

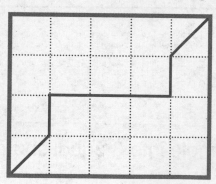

_____

_____

_____

12. **Assessment** Meg divides a rectangle into 3 equal shares that are **NOT** the same shape. Which could be Meg's rectangle?

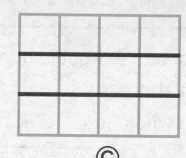

Ⓐ

Ⓒ

Ⓑ

Ⓓ

Help   Tools   Games

Another Look!

You can divide a rectangle into equal shares in different ways.

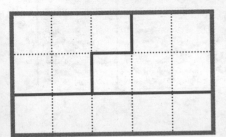  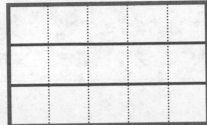

Each equal share has 5 squares.

HOME ACTIVITY Draw a rectangle. Ask your child to divide it into two equal shares that have different shapes.

Each rectangle has 3 equal shares. Each equal share has 5 squares.

Draw lines to show three different ways to divide the same rectangle into 2 equal shares.

1.

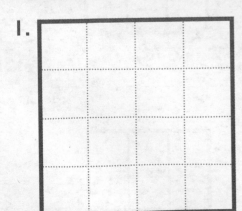 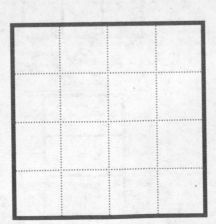 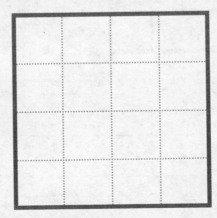

Can you divide a rectangle into equal shares that have DIFFERENT shapes?

Solve each problem.

2. **Explain** Lexi wants to share the sheet of tiger stickers with two friends. Are there enough stickers to make equal shares for Lexi and her two friends? Explain.

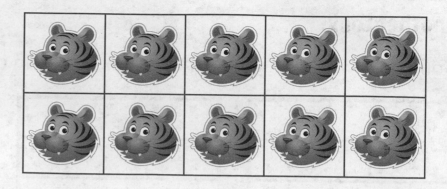

_____

_____

_____

3. **Higher Order Thinking** Corbin drew lines in this rectangle to make equal shares. How do you know that each share is **NOT** a third of the whole rectangle?

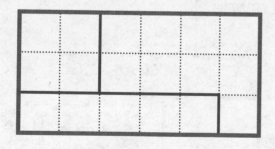

_____

_____

4. ✓**Assessment** Lynn divides a rectangle into 3 equal shares. Which could **NOT** be Lynn's rectangle?

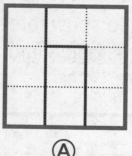
Ⓐ

Ⓒ

Ⓑ

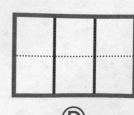
Ⓓ

Tools Assessment

Independent Practice ☆ Solve each problem. Use crayons to color. Explain your work.

2. Marie wants to put a rectangular design on a T-shirt. The design must have 4 colors with an equal share for each color. Create two possible designs for Marie.

Design 1 **Design 2**

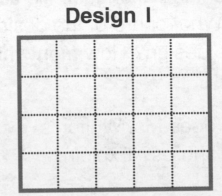

_____

_____

_____

_____

3. Grant wants to put a circle design on his toy car. The design must have 3 colors with an equal share for each color. Create two possible designs for Grant.

Design 1 **Design 2**

_____

_____

_____

_____

Problem Solving

Tile Design

Ms. Walton created this rectangular tile design. What share of the design is orange? What share of the design is yellow? How many shares is the whole design? How many thirds is the whole?

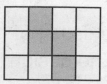

4. Make Sense How does Ms. Walton's design show equal shares? Explain.

_____

_____

_____

5. Reasoning What share of the design is orange? What share of the design is yellow? How many shares is the whole design? How many thirds is the whole?

_____

_____

_____

_____

6. Generalize Copy the tile design above onto this grid. Then color it orange and yellow to match the design shown above.

How did you copy the design? Describe one or two shortcuts you used.

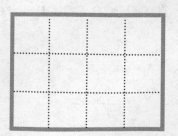

_____

Help Tools Games

Another Look! Create two different designs for these squares that are the same size. Each design needs to have 2 colors with an equal share for each color.

I can draw a line down the center to make equal shares.

I can draw a line from opposite corners to make equal shares.

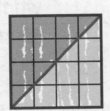

Design 1

Design 2

Design 2 also has equal shares that are the same shape.

HOME ACTIVITY Draw two identical rectangles. Have your child use crayons to draw a different design in each rectangle. Each rectangle should show 4 equal shares, each in a different color.

Solve the problem. Use crayons to color. Explain your solution.

1. Make two different designs. Each design must have 3 colors with an equal share for each color. One design should have shares that are NOT all the same shape.

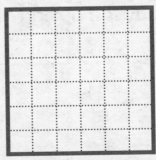

Design 1

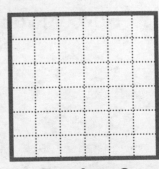

Design 2

_____

_____

A Design Repeated

Steven created this design on 4 squares of grid paper.
He wants to repeat this design 6 times on a larger grid.
Answer the questions to help Steven create the larger design.

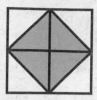

2. **Look for Patterns** Look at each small square of Steven's design. How are they alike? How are they different?

_____

_____

_____

_____

3. **Explain** Describe Steven's design. Explain what it looks like. Use *half of, a third of*, or *a fourth of* when you describe it.

_____

_____

_____

_____

4. **Generalize** Copy Steven's design 4 times.
Use 2 colors. Put 2 designs next to each other in each row.

How did you copy the design? Describe a shortcut you used.

_____

_____

_____

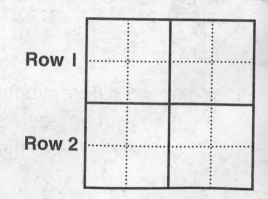

Row 1

Row 2

Name _____

Follow the Path

Find each sum or difference. Then color a path from **Start** to **Finish**. Follow the sums and differences that are even numbers. You can only move up, down, right, or left.

I can ...
add and subtract within 100.

Start								
69 − 23	31 + 25	78 − 47	97 − 49	72 + 12	76 − 38	67 − 47	48 + 24	46 + 37
84 − 61	73 − 55	68 + 29	11 + 17	37 + 58	86 − 51	21 + 38	82 − 18	81 − 62
43 + 42	27 + 49	35 + 48	46 − 32	73 − 26	30 + 31	46 − 28	47 + 41	62 − 39
25 + 16	60 − 36	50 − 29	39 + 43	60 − 45	64 + 23	29 + 35	56 + 41	94 − 61
35 + 42	85 − 23	24 + 56	58 + 36	97 − 38	25 − 16	38 + 62	79 − 49	59 + 23

Finish

A·Z Glossary

Word List
- angle
- cube
- edge
- equal shares
- face
- fourths
- halves
- hexagon
- pentagon
- polygon
- quadrilateral
- right angle
- thirds
- vertex

Understand Vocabulary

Write *always*, *sometimes*, or *never*.

1. A cube has exactly 4 faces. _____

2. A right angle forms a square corner. _____

3. Quadrilaterals are squares. _____

4. A solid figure with faces has edges. _____

Draw a line from each term to its example.

5. hexagon

6. pentagon

7. vertex

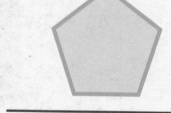

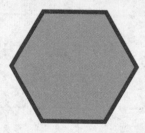

Use Vocabulary in Writing

8. Tell how you can divide a square into two equal shares. Then tell how you can divide that same square into 3 equal shares. Use terms from the Word List.

Name _____

Set A

You can name a plane shape by its number of sides and vertices.

vertex

side

_3_ sides

_3_ vertices

Shape: triangle

_4_ sides

_4_ vertices

Shape:

quadrilateral

Write the number of sides and vertices. Name the shape.

1.

_____ sides

_____ vertices

Shape: _____

2.

_____ sides

_____ vertices

Shape: _____

Set B

You can name a polygon by the number of its angles.

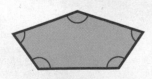

_5_ angles

pentagon

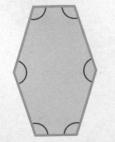

_6_ angles

hexagon

Write the number of angles. Then name the shape.

3.

_____ angles

Shape: _____

4.

_____ angles

Shape: _____

You can draw a polygon with a given number of sides, vertices, or angles.

Draw a polygon with 4 sides that are different lengths.

Draw a polygon with 5 vertices.

Draw a polygon with 3 angles. One angle is a right angle.

Draw each polygon described.

5. 6 sides

6. 3 vertices

7. 5 sides and 2 right angles

8. 8 angles

You can describe and draw cubes.

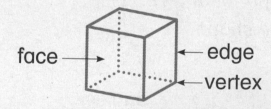

face → ← edge
← vertex

Every cube has ___6___ faces,

___12___ edges, and ___8___ vertices.

9. Cross out the shapes that are **NOT** cubes.

10. Draw a cube. Use the dots to help you.

Name _____

Set E _____

You can cover a rectangle with squares.

column

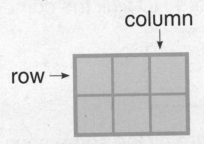

row →

Count by rows: $3 + 3 = 6$

Count by columns: $2 + 2 + 2 = 6$

___6___ squares cover the rectangle.

Use square tiles to cover the rectangle. Trace the tiles. Then count the squares.

11.

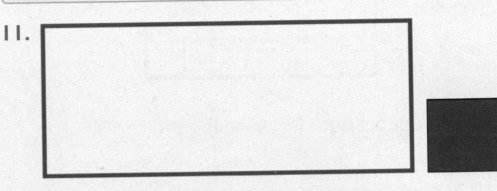

_____ squares cover the rectangle.

Set F _____

You can divide circles and rectangles into equal shares.

2 equal shares are **halves**.

3 equal shares are **thirds**.

4 equal shares are **fourths**.

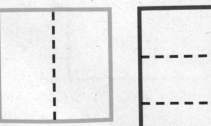

Divide each shape into the given number of equal shares. Show 2 ways.

12. halves

13. thirds

14. fourths

Equal shares can be different shapes.

This is one way to divide this rectangle

into ⋯3⋯ equal shares.

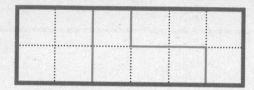

Each equal share is ⋯4⋯ squares.

Thinking Habits

Repeated Reasoning

Does something repeat in the problem?

How can the solution help me solve another problem?

Draw lines to show two more ways to divide the rectangle into 3 equal shares.

15. equal shares that are **NOT** all the same shape

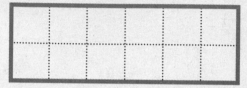

16. equal shares that are all the same shape

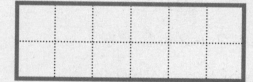

Use the design shown. Create a different design with 3 equal shares.

17.

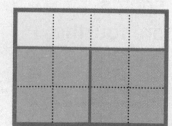 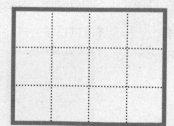

Name _____

1. Which polygons are pentagons? Choose all that apply.

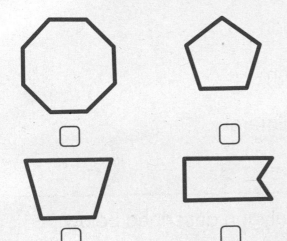

2. Rita draws a polygon. It has fewer than 8 sides and more angles than a square. Which shape did Rita draw?

Ⓐ triangle

Ⓑ rectangle

Ⓒ hexagon

Ⓓ quadrilateral

3. Which rectangles are divided into fourths? Choose all that apply.

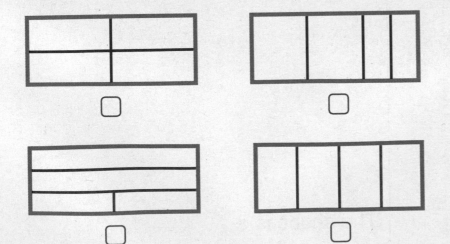

4. Draw a polygon with 4 angles. Make one angle a right angle. Then name the polygon.

Name: _____

nine hundred thirteen **913**

5. Is the polygon a quadrilateral?
Choose Yes or No.

I have 3 sides and 3 angles. ○ Yes ○ No

I have 4 sides and 4 angles. ○ Yes ○ No

I am a square. ○ Yes ○ No

I am a rectangle. ○ Yes ○ No

6. Mandy draws a polygon with 6 sides and 6 angles. Which shape did she draw?

Ⓐ pentagon

Ⓑ hexagon

Ⓒ octagon

Ⓓ quadrilateral

7. Name the shape below. Write 3 things that describe the shape.

8. Draw the polygon described below. Then complete the sentence.

I have 2 fewer sides than a pentagon.
I have 1 less angle than a square.
I have one right angle.

The shape is a _____.

9. Complete the sentence to name and describe the solid figure below.

A _____ has _____ faces, _____ vertices,

and _____ edges.

10. Divide the circle into 2 equal shares. Then complete the sentences.

Each share is a _____ of the whole.

The whole is _____ halves.

11. Brad says there are only two ways to divide the same rectangle below into 3 equal shares. Do you agree? Use words and pictures to explain.

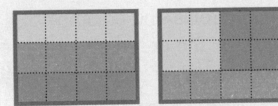

12. Count the number of squares in the rows and columns of the rectangle. Use the numbers on the cards to write the missing numbers in the equations.

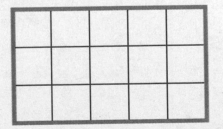

| 15 | 3 | 5 |

Rows: _____ + _____ + _____ = _____ squares

Columns: _____ + _____ + _____ + _____ + _____ = _____ squares

13. Kerry wants a design that shows thirds. Which designs could Kerry use? Choose all that apply.

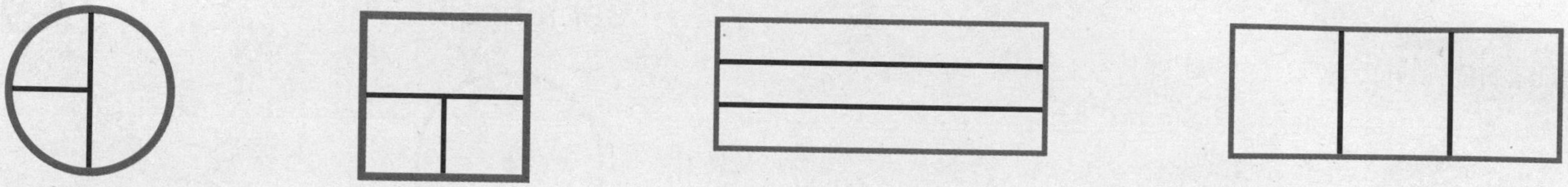

☐   ☐   ☐   ☐

14. Is the solid figure a cube? Choose Yes or No.

☐ Yes ☐ No   ☐ Yes ☐ No   ☐ Yes ☐ No   ☐ Yes ☐ No

15. Use the dot paper.
Draw a cube.

16. Divide the rectangle into rows and columns of squares the same size as the green square. Then count the squares.

_____ squares

Name _____

Happy Home

Tina and her family moved into a new home.
They bought different things for each room.

1. They hang pictures on the wall.
   Name the shape of each picture frame.

_____

_____

2. The rug in the kitchen has
   5 sides and 5 vertices.
   Draw the shape of the rug.

   Name the shape. _____

3. The wallpaper uses this pattern.

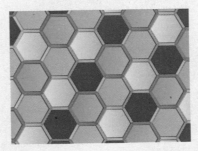

   Name the shape in the pattern.

   _____

   Write the number of sides, vertices, and
   angles in the shape.

   _____ sides   _____ vertices   _____ angles

4. The living room has 2 end tables.

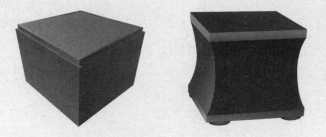

Circle the table that is a cube. Explain.

_____

_____

_____

_____

5. Tina has a new quilt for her bed. Her quilt has this design.

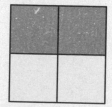

What share is green? _____

What share is yellow? _____

6. Tina's mother is making a quilt made of smaller squares. She wants the quilt to have 4 colors. Each color has an equal share.

Part A

Use 4 colors to make a possible quilt design below. Make the equal shares the same shape.

Design 1

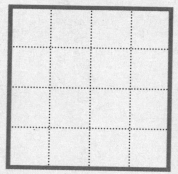

Part B

Use 4 colors to make a different quilt design below. Make the equal shares have different shapes.

Design 2

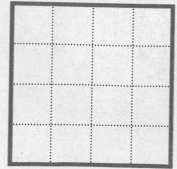

Here's a preview of next year. These lessons help you step up to Grade 3.

STEP UP to Grade 3

Lessons

Grade 3 lessons look different. Rotate the pages so your name is at the top.

Solve

Lesson 1

Multiplication as Repeated Addition

I can...
use addition or multiplication to join equal groups.

I can also make sense of problems.

Name _____

☆ **Solve & Share** ☆

Ms. Witt bought 3 boxes of paint with 5 jars of paint in each box. What is the total number of jars Ms. Witt bought? *Solve this problem any way you choose.*

Make sense of this problem. Think about what you know and what you need to find.

Look Back! **Model with Math** How can you use a picture to show the math you did in the problem?

Digital Resources at SavvasRealize.com

How Can You Find the Total Number of Objects in Equal Groups?

A

Jessie used 3 bags to bring home the goldfish she won at the Fun Fair. She put the same number of goldfish in each bag. How many goldfish did she win?

I can use counters to show the groups.

8 goldfish in each bag

B

The counters show 3 groups of 8 goldfish.

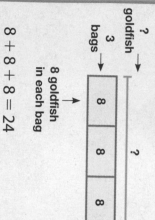

You can use addition to join equal groups.

goldfish →

3 bags →

| 8 | 8 | 8 |

?

8 goldfish in each bag

8 + 8 + 8 = 24

C

Multiplication is an operation that gives the total number when you join equal groups.

goldfish →

3 bags →

| 8 | 8 | 8 |

?

8 goldfish in each bag

3 times 8 equals 24

3 × 8 = 24

factor factor product

Factors are the numbers that are being multiplied. The product is the answer to a multiplication problem.

D

You can write equations. Use a question mark for the unknown number that you find.

Addition equation:
8 + 8 + 8 = ?
8 + 8 + 8 = 24

Multiplication equation:
3 × 8 = ?
3 × 8 = 24

Jessie won 24 goldfish.

Convince Me! Model with Math Suppose Jessie won 5 bags of 8 goldfish. Draw a bar diagram and write an addition equation and a multiplication equation to represent the problem.

Name _____

☆ Guided Practice ☆

Do You Understand?

1. Reasoning Can you write
$3 + 3 + 3 + 3 = 12$ as a multiplication equation? Explain.

2. Reasoning Can you write
$1 + 5 + 7 = 13$ as a multiplication equation? Explain.

3. Write an addition equation and a multiplication equation to solve this problem.
Matt buys 3 bags of apples. There are 6 apples in each bag. How many apples does Matt buy?

Do You Know How?

Complete **4** and **5**. Use the pictures to help.

4.

2 groups of _____

$3 + 3 =$ _____

$2 \times$ _____ $=$ _____

5.

_____ groups of 2

$2 +$ _____ $+$ _____ $=$ _____

$3 \times$ _____ $=$ _____

☆ Independent Practice ☆

Complete **6** and **7**. Use the pictures to help.

6.

2 groups of _____

$4 +$ _____ $=$ _____

$2 \times$ _____ $=$ _____

7.

3 groups of _____

$4 +$ _____ $+$ _____ $=$ _____

$3 \times$ _____ $=$ _____

In **8–11**, complete each equation. Use counters or draw a picture to help.

8. $5 + 5 + 5 + 5 = 4 \times$ _____

9. _____ $+$ _____ $= 2 \times 7$

10. $9 +$ _____ $= 2 \times$ _____

11. $6 + 6 + 6 + 6 =$ _____ $\times$ _____

Problem Solving ☆

12. Model with Math Lily has 8 eggs. Draw pictures to show two different ways Lily can make equal groups using 8 eggs.

13. Be Precise Erin reads 54 pages of her book. The book has 93 pages in all. How many pages does Erin have left to read? Show your work.

_____ pages

---

14. Critique Reasoning Chris says she can write two different equations to show 15 as repeated addition. Is Chris correct? Why or why not?

15. Higher Order Thinking George says you need equal groups to multiply. Is George correct? Why or why not?

◀ **Assessment**

16. Zoey has 10 stickers. She puts them in 2 groups of 5. How can you represent this? Choose all that apply.

☐ $5 + 2$

☐ $2 + 2 + 2 + 2 + 2$

☐ $5 + 5$

☐ 2×5

☐ $10 + 2 + 5$

17. Drew earns $6 each week. He wants to know how much money he will have saved after 5 weeks. How can you represent this? Choose all that apply.

☐ $6 + $6 + $6 + $6 + $6

☐ $6 \times 6

☐ $6 + $6

☐ $5 + $5 + $5 + $5 + $5

☐ $6 \times 5

924

Lesson 2

Arrays and Multiplication

I can... use arrays to show and solve multiplication problems.

I can also use math tools correctly.

Name _____

Solve & Share

Mark put sports cards in an album. He put 4 rows of cards on each page. He put 3 cards in each row. How many cards are on each page? *Solve this problem any way you choose.*

Solve

You can use tools. Sometimes using objects can help you solve a problem. Show your work in the space below!

Look Back! Make Sense and Persevere Will your answer be the same if Mark puts 3 rows of 4 cards on each page? Explain.

Essential Question

How Does an Array Show Multiplication?

A

Dana keeps her swimming medal collection in a display on the wall.

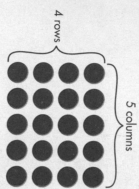

The display has 4 rows. Each row has 5 medals. How many medals are in Dana's collection?

The medals are in an array. An array shows objects in equal rows and columns.

B

The counters show 4 rows and 5 columns.

4 rows
5 columns

Each row is a group. You can use addition or skip counting to find the total.

Addition: 5 + 5 + 5 + 5 = 20
Skip counting: 5, 10, 15, 20

C

Multiplication can also be used to find the total in an array.

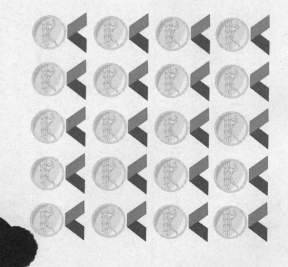

You say, "4 times 5 equals 20."

$$4 \times 5 = 20$$

number of rows

number in each row

There are 20 medals in Dana's collection.

Convince Me! Construct Arguments Jason also has a swimming medal collection. His display has 5 rows with 5 medals in each row. Who has more medals, Jason or Dana? Draw an array, then write an addition equation and a multiplication equation to show your work.

Name _____

☆ Guided Practice ☆

Do You Understand?

1. Look at page 926. What does the second factor tell you about the array?

2. Gina puts muffins in 4 rows with 8 muffins in each row. Draw an array to find the total number of muffins.

Do You Know How?

In **3** and **4**, write a multiplication equation for each array.

3.

4.

☆ Independent Practice ☆

In **5–7**, write a multiplication equation for each array.

5.

6.

7.

In **8** and **9**, draw an array to show each equation. Write the product.

8. $5 \times 9 =$ _____

9. $2 \times 8 =$ _____

Problem Solving ☆

10. **Look for Relationships** Lance draws these two arrays. How are the arrays alike? How are they different?

11. **Construct Arguments** How many more birch trees are there than pine trees? Explain how you know.

DATA		
Trees in the Park		
Birch	⫲⫲ 𝙸	
Oak	///	
Maple	⫲⫲	
Pine	//	

12. **Higher Order Thinking** Rachel has 19 pictures. Can she use all the pictures to make an array with exactly 4 equal rows? Why or why not?

13. Larry puts 7 nickels in each of his 3 empty piggy banks. How many nickels does Larry put in the banks? Write a multiplication equation to show how you solved the problem.

? nickels

| 7 | 7 | 7 |

3 piggy banks →   ← 7 nickels in each bank

◀ **Assessment**

14. Mr. Williams planted 6 rows of apple trees on his farm. The apple trees are in 8 columns. How many trees are there in all?

   Ⓐ 6
   Ⓑ 8
   Ⓒ 14
   Ⓓ 48

15. Tina bought the stickers shown below. Which of the following shows how many stickers Tina bought?

   Ⓐ 5 + 2
   Ⓑ 5 × 2
   Ⓒ 5 × 5
   Ⓓ 5 − 2

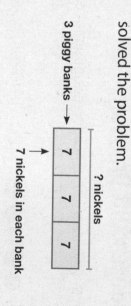

There are 5 rows. There are 2 stickers in each row.

928

Name _____

Solve & Share

Four friends picked 20 apples. They want to share them equally. How many apples should each person get? **Solve this problem any way you choose.**

Solve

Lesson 3
Division as Sharing

I can ...
use objects or pictures to show how objects can be divided into equal groups.

I can also model with math.

Model with math.
Drawing a picture that represents the problem can help you solve it.
Show your work!

Look Back! **Use Appropriate Tools** Can you use counters to help you solve this problem? Explain.

930

Essential Question How Many Are in Each Group?

A

Three friends have 12 toys to share equally.
How many toys will each friend get?

Think of arranging 12 toys into 3 equal groups.

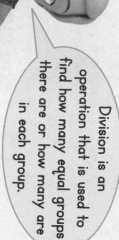

Division is an operation that is used to find how many equal groups there are or how many are in each group.

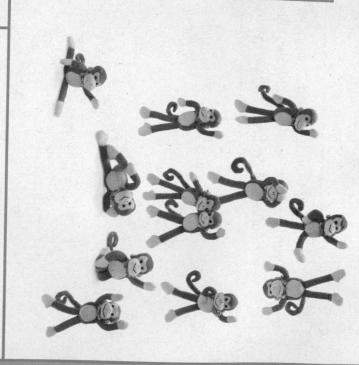

B

What You Think
Put one toy at a time in each group.

12 toys

4 toys for each friend

When all the toys are grouped, there will be 4 in each group.

C

What You Write
You can write a division equation to find the number in each group.

12 ÷ 3 = 4

Total → 12
Number of equal groups → 3
Number in each group → 4

Each friend will get 4 toys.

Convince Me! **Be Precise** What would happen if 3 friends wanted to share 13 toys equally?

Lesson 4

Division as Repeated Subtraction

I can...
use repeated subtraction to understand and solve division problems.

I can also reason about math.

Solve

Name _____

☆ **Solve & Share** ☆

Li made 12 tacos. He wants to give some of his friends 2 tacos each. If Li does not get any of the tacos, how many of his friends will get tacos? *Solve this problem any way you choose.*

You can use reasoning. How can what you know about sharing help you solve the problem? Show your work in the space below!

Look Back! **Use Appropriate Tools** How can counters or other objects help you show your work?

How Can You Divide Using Repeated Subtraction?

A

June has 10 strawberries to serve to her guests. If each guest eats 2 strawberries, how many guests can June serve?

10 strawberries →

2

10

? guests

2 strawberries for each guest

B

You can use repeated subtraction to find how many groups of 2 are in 10.

$10 - 2 = 8$
$8 - 2 = 6$
$6 - 2 = 4$
$4 - 2 = 2$
$2 - 2 = 0$

You can subtract 2 five times. There are five groups of 2 in 10. There are no strawberries left.

June can serve 5 guests.

C

You can write a division equation to find the number of groups.

Write: $10 \div 2 = ?$
Read: Ten divided by 2 equals what number?
Solve: $10 \div 2 = 5$

June can serve 5 guests.

Convince Me! Model with Math In the example above, what if each guest eats 5 strawberries? Use the math you know to represent the problem and find how many guests June could serve.

☆ Guided Practice ☆

Do You Understand?

1. Show how you can use repeated subtraction to find how many groups of 5 there are in 25. Then write a division equation to solve the problem.

Do You Know How?

In **2** and **3**, use counters or draw a picture to solve.

2. The basketball team has 14 shoes. There are 2 shoes in each pair. How many pairs of shoes are there?

3. Maya has 18 cat toys. She gives each of her cats 6 toys. How many cats does Maya have?

☆ Independent Practice ☆

In **4** and **5**, complete the equations.

4. Tanya picks 18 pears. She places 9 pears in each bag. How many bags does Tanya have?

$18 - 9 =$ ___

___ $- 9 =$ ___

___ $\div 9 =$ ___

Tanya has ___ bags.

5. The workers on a farm have 7 keys each. There are 21 keys. How many workers are on the farm?

$21 - 7 =$ ___

___ $- 7 =$ ___

___ $-$ ___ $=$ ___

___ $\div$ ___ $=$ ___

There are ___ workers.

In **6** and **7**, use counters or draw a picture to solve.

6. Shawna bought 36 markers that came in packages of 4 markers each. How many packages did Shawna buy?

7. James has 16 pencils. He puts 2 pencils on each desk. How many desks are there?

Problem Solving

8. Generalize The chart shows the number of pennies each of three friends has in her pocket. Each friend divides her money into piles of 4 coins. Write division equations to show how many equal piles each friend can make. Explain what repeats in the equations and how it helps you solve.

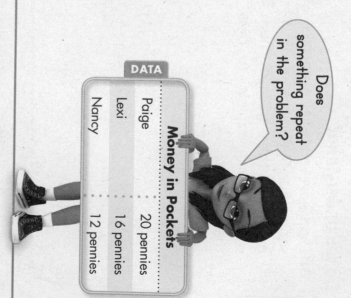

Does something repeat in the problem?

DATA

Money in Pockets

Paige	20 pennies
Lexi	16 pennies
Nancy	12 pennies

9. If Lexi makes 8 columns of pennies, how many rows does she make? Write an equation to model and solve the problem.

10. Model with Math Tim has $45. He spends $21, then finds $28. How much money does Tim have now? Use math to represent the problem.

11. Higher Order Thinking A bakery plans to make 8 new muffins each year. How many years will it take for the store to make 40 new muffins? Write and solve an equation.

❮ Assessment

12. Andy writes the following:

$$8 - 4 = 4$$
$$4 - 4 = 0$$

Which equation could Andy use to represent the same problem?

Ⓐ $4 \times 4 = 16$

Ⓑ $8 \div 8 = 1$

Ⓒ $8 \div 4 = 2$

Ⓓ $4 \div 2 = 2$

13. Rae writes the following:

$$27 - 9 = 18$$
$$18 - 9 = 9$$
$$9 - 9 = 0$$

Which problem is Rae trying to solve?

Ⓐ $27 \div 9$

Ⓑ $27 \div 3$

Ⓒ $27 - 9$

Ⓓ 27×3

Lesson 5
Add with
Partial Sums

I can . . .
add numbers using partial sums.

I can also reason about math.

Solve

Name _____

★ Solve & Share ★

Find the sum of 327 + 241. Think about place value. **Solve this problem any way you choose.**

You can use reasoning to make a plan. Part of your plan for solving this problem could be to show each of the numbers in expanded form. Show your work in the space below!

Look Back! Reasoning How can using place value help you solve this 3-digit addition problem?

How Can You Break Large Addition Problems into Smaller Ones?

A

Find the sum of 243 + 179. Each digit in the numbers can be modeled with place-value blocks.

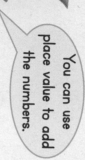

You can use place value to add the numbers.

243

179

B

Step 1

Break 243 + 179 into smaller problems. Think about the place value of each number.

Hundreds	Tens	Ones
200	40	3
+ 100	+ 70	+ 9
300	110	12

C

Step 2

Then, add the sums of all the places.

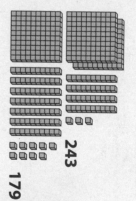

```
  300
  110
+  12
  422
```

So, 243 + 179 = 422.

Convince Me! Construct Arguments Lexi says, "To solve 243 + 179, I can just count on with place-value blocks to find the answer: 100, 200, 300, another hundred from the 11 tens is 400, one more ten and 12 ones is 422!" How is Lexi's way like Steps 1 and 2 above?

938

☆ Guided Practice ☆

Do You Understand?

1. Reasoning Suppose you are adding 824 + 106. What would the tens problem be? Why?

2. Write the smaller problems you could use to find 512 + 362. What is the sum?

Do You Know How?

In **3**, use place value to find the sum.

3.

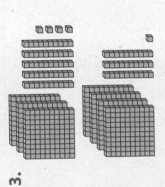

Find 354 + 431.

Hundreds	Tens	Ones	Total
300	50	4	
+400	+30	+1	

☆ Independent Practice ☆

In **4** through **11**, find each sum.

4.

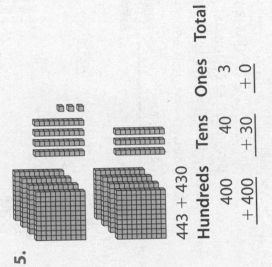

348 + 131

Hundreds	Tens	Ones	Total
300	40	8	
+100	+30	+1	

5.

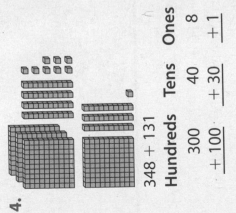

443 + 430

Hundreds	Tens	Ones	Total
400	40	3	
+400	+30	+0	

6. 264 + 524

7. 541 + 276

8. 249 + 180

9. 342 + 168

10. 191 + 502

11. 473 + 405

Problem Solving ☆

12. Critique Reasoning Henry believes the sum of 345 + 124 is 479. Is Henry correct? Explain.

345	124

?

13. Construct Arguments Explain how the solids shown in Group A and Group B could have been sorted.

Group A   Group B

14. Model with Math Bill needs to find 325 + 133. Into what three smaller problems can Bill break this addition? What is the sum?

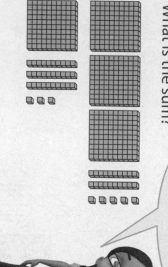

You can use place value to add.

15. Higher Order Thinking A school cafeteria sells 215 lunches on Monday, 104 lunches on Tuesday, and 262 lunches on Wednesday. Did the cafeteria sell more lunches on Monday and Tuesday or on Tuesday and Wednesday? Explain.

Assessment

16. Jan read a book with 288 pages. Lara read a book with 416 pages. How many pages did Jan and Lara both read? Solve using partial sums.

Ⓐ 694
Ⓑ 704
Ⓒ 706
Ⓓ 716

17. Cody wants to add 482 + 315. He writes (400 + 300) + (80 + 10) + (2 + 5). Which shows the sum of the hundreds, tens, and ones?

Ⓐ 700 + 90 + 5
Ⓑ 700 + 90 + 7
Ⓒ 800 + 80 + 5
Ⓓ 800 + 60 + 7

Name _____

Solve & Share

☆ ☆

Find the sum of 146 + 247.

Solve this problem any way you choose.

Solve

Lesson 6

Models for Adding 3-Digit Numbers

I can ...
add 3-digit numbers using models, drawings, and place value.

I can also model with math.

Model with math. You can use place-value blocks and draw pictures of the blocks to show how you found the sum. Show your work!

Look Back! **Generalize** When you add numbers, how do you know if you need to regroup?

Essential
Question

How Can You Add 3-Digit Numbers with Place-Value Blocks?

A

Find 143 + 285.

You can add whole numbers by using place value to break them apart.

143

285

B

Add the ones, tens, and hundreds.

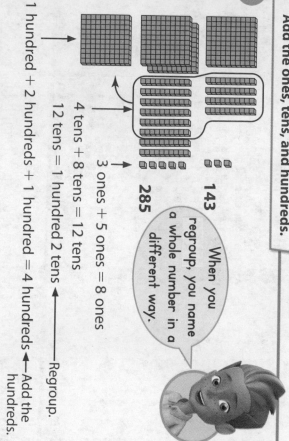

143

285

When you regroup, you name a whole number in a different way.

3 ones + 5 ones = 8 ones

4 tens + 8 tens = 12 tens

12 tens = 1 hundred 2 tens ← Regroup.

1 hundred + 2 hundreds + 1 hundred = 4 hundreds ← Add the hundreds.

C

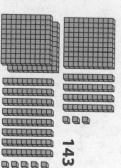

4 hundreds   2 tens   8 ones

428

143 + 285 = 428

Convince Me! Model with Math Mr. Wu drove 224 miles yesterday. He drove 175 miles today. Use place-value blocks or draw pictures of blocks to find how many miles Mr. Wu drove.

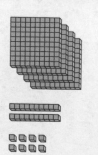

Tools

Another Example!

You may have to regroup twice when you add. Find 148 + 276.

Step 1

Add the ones.

8 ones + 6 ones = 14 ones

Regroup.

14 ones = 1 ten 4 ones

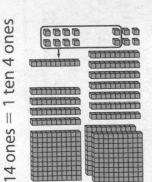

Step 2

Add the tens.

1 ten + 4 tens + 7 tens = 12 tens

Regroup.

12 tens = 1 hundred 2 tens

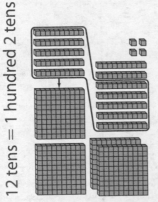
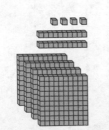

Step 3

Add the hundreds.

1 hundred + 1 hundred +
2 hundreds = 4 hundreds

So, 148 + 276 = 424.

☆ Guided Practice ☆

Do You Understand?

1. **Generalize** How do you know when you need to regroup?

2. **Use Appropriate Tools** Use place-value blocks to find 136 + 279.

Do You Know How?

In **3**, use the model to write the problem and find the sum.

3.

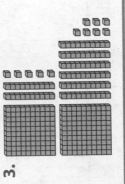

☆ Independent Practice ☆

In **4** through **6**, write the problem and find the sum.

4.

5.

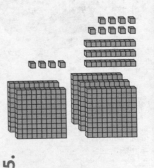

6.

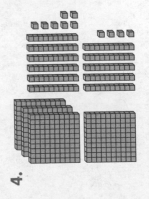

7. Model with Math Juan wants to use place-value blocks to show 148 + 256. Draw a picture of the blocks Juan should use. What is the sum?

8. Use Appropriate Tools Manuel plays basketball and scores 15 points in game one, 8 points in game two, and 17 points in game three. How many points did Manuel score? Use the number line to solve the problem.

```
 ┃━━┿━┿━┿━┿━┿━┿━┿━┿━┿━┿━┿━▶
   0  10 20 30 40 50
```

9. Construct Arguments Al and Mark were playing a computer game. Al scored 265 points in the first round and scored 352 points in the second round. Mark scored 354 points in the second round. Mark scored 237 points in the first round and scored more points and won the game? Who scored more points and won the game? Explain.

10. Higher Order Thinking Paula is saving money to buy a new computer that costs $680. Last month she saved $415, and this month she saved $298. Does Paula have enough money saved to buy the computer? Use place-value blocks to help you solve the problem. Explain.

< Assessment

11. Write an equation that represents what the place-value blocks show.

You may have to regroup when you find the sum.

12. Mrs. Samuels bought a $526 plane ticket in May and a $194 plane ticket in June. Use place-value blocks or draw pictures to find out how much Mrs. Samuels spent on both of the plane tickets.

Lesson 7
Subtract with Partial Differences

I can . . . subtract numbers using partial differences.

I can also reason about math.

Solve

Name _____

Solve & Share

Find the difference of 534 − 108. Think about place value. *Solve this problem any way you choose.*

You can use reasoning. How could you break this problem into smaller subtraction problems? Show your work in the space below!

Look Back! Reasoning How can using place value help you solve this subtraction problem?

Essential
Question

How Can You Break Large Subtraction Problems into Smaller Ones?

A

At the end of the fourth round of a game of Digit Derby, Marco's score was 462 points. During the fifth round of the game, Marco loses points. What is Marco's score at the end of the fifth round?

Find 462 − 181.

Place value can help you break a subtraction problem into smaller problems.

End of Round 4

Marco has 462 points.

End of Round 5

Marco loses 181 points.

B

Step 1

Start with 462.

Subtract the **hundreds**.

$462 - 100 = 362$

So far, 100 has been subtracted.

C

Step 2

Next, start with 362.

Subtract the **tens**.

You need to subtract 8 tens, but there are not enough tens. So, subtract the 6 tens.

$362 - 60 = 302$

Then, subtract the 2 tens that are left.

$302 - 20 = 282$

So far, $100 + 60 + 20 = 180$ has been subtracted.

D

Step 3

That leaves just 1 to subtract.

Subtract the **ones**.

$282 - 1 = 281$

$100 + 60 + 20 + 1 = 181$ has been subtracted.

At the end of the fifth round, Marco's score is 281 points.

Convince Me! **Use Structure** Find 453 − 262. Use place value to help break the problem into smaller problems. Show your work.

Name _____

☆ Guided Practice

Do You Understand?

1. Construct Arguments Why do you need to record the numbers you subtract at each step?

2. Reasoning Carmella is trying to find 784 − 310. She decides to start by subtracting 10 from 784. Do you agree with Carmella? Explain.

Do You Know How?

In **3** and **4**, use place value to help break the problem into smaller problems.

3. Find 564 − 346.

564 − 300 = _____

264 − 40 = _____

224 − 4 = _____

220 − 2 = _____

4. Find 769 − 375.

769 − 300 = _____

469 − 60 = _____

409 − 10 = _____

399 − 5 = _____

☆ Independent Practice ☆

In **5** through **10**, follow the steps to find each difference. Show your work.

5. 728 − 413

First, subtract 400.

_____ − _____ = 328

Then, subtract 10.

_____ − _____ = _____

Then, subtract 3.

_____ − 3 = _____

6. 936 − 524

First, subtract 500.

936 − _____ = _____

Then, subtract 20.

_____ − 20 = _____

Then, subtract 4.

_____ − _____ = _____

7. 854 − 235

First, subtract 200.

_____ − 200 = _____

Then, subtract 30.

_____ − 30 = _____

Then, subtract 4.

_____ − _____ = _____

Then, subtract 1.

_____ − 1 = _____

8. 955 − 283

9. 946 − 507

10. 984 − 356

Step Up | Lesson 7 **947**

Problem Solving

11. Use Appropriate Tools Write the time shown on the clock in 2 different ways.

12. Use Structure There are 96 boys and 83 girls in the school lunchroom. Near the end of lunch, 127 students leave. How many students are left in the lunchroom? Show how you can break part of the problem into smaller problems.

13. Model with Math Yuki had a necklace with 131 beads. The string broke, and she lost 43 beads. How many beads does Yuki have left?

131 beads

43	?

43 beads lost →   ? beads left →

14. Higher Order Thinking Which weighs more, two adult male Basset Hounds or one adult male Great Dane? Show the difference in pounds between the two Basset Hounds and the Great Dane. Draw bar diagrams to represent and help you solve the problem.

Great Dane   Basset Hound

145 pounds

66 pounds

Assessment

15. Karl's book has 416 pages. He read 50 pages last week. He read another 31 pages this week. How many more pages does Karl have left to read?

Ⓐ 125

Ⓑ 245

Ⓒ 335

Ⓓ 345

You can break the problem into smaller problems to solve.

948

Name _____

☆ ☆ Solve & Share

Solve

Find the difference of 246 — 153.
Solve this problem any way you choose.

> Model with math.
> Drawing pictures of place-value blocks is one way to represent this problem and help you solve it. Show your work!

Lesson 8

Models for Subtracting 3-Digit Numbers

I can ... subtract 3-digit numbers using models, drawings, and place value.

I can also model with math.

Look Back! Generalize How can you check your answer for 246 — 153?

How Can You Subtract 3-Digit Numbers with Place-Value Blocks?

A

Fish caught near the Hawaiian Islands can be very large. How many more pounds does a broadbill swordfish weigh than a blue marlin?

Find 237 − 165.

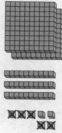

Use place value to subtract the ones first, the tens next, and then the hundreds.

DATA

Wild Hawaiian Fish Weights

Type of Fish	Weight (in lb)
Blue Marlin	165
Broadbill Swordfish	237

Show 237 with place-value blocks.

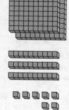

B

Subtract the ones.

7 ones > 5 ones, so no regrouping.

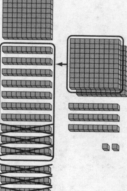

7 ones − 5 ones = 2 ones

$$\begin{array}{r} 237 \\ -\ 165 \\ \hline 2 \end{array}$$

C

Subtract the tens.

3 tens < 6 tens, so regroup.

1 hundred = 10 tens

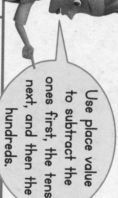

13 tens − 6 tens = 7 tens

$$\begin{array}{r} \overset{1\ 13}{2\cancel{3}7} \\ -\ 165 \\ \hline 72 \end{array}$$

D

Subtract the hundreds.

1 hundred − 1 hundred = 0 hundreds

$$\begin{array}{r} \overset{1\ 13}{2\cancel{3}7} \\ -\ 165 \\ \hline 72 \end{array}$$

So, 237 − 165 = 72. A broadbill swordfish weighs 72 more pounds than a blue marlin.

Convince Me! Model with Math Anderson needs $231 to buy a new bike. He saved $144 from his summer job. How much more does Anderson need to save to buy the bike? Write a subtraction equation that models the problem. Use place-value blocks to help you solve the problem using the same steps shown above.

☆ Guided Practice

Do You Understand?

1. Generalize In the example on page 950, for 237 − 165, why do you need to regroup 1 hundred into 10 tens?

2. Model with Math Gary saved $287 doing jobs in his neighborhood. He bought a computer printer for $183. How much money did Gary have left? Draw a picture of place-value blocks to help you subtract.

Do You Know How?

In **3** through **10**, use place-value blocks or draw pictures to subtract.

3. 859
     − 768

4. 361
     − 124

5. 285
     − 49

6. 684
     − 482

7. 384 − 358

8. 352 − 214

9. 512 − 101

10. 999 − 889

☆ Independent Practice ☆

In **11** through **22**, use place-value blocks or draw pictures to subtract.

You can draw squares to show hundreds, lines to show tens, and dots to show ones. This picture shows 123.

▢ ‖ ∴

11. 651
     − 543

12. 492
     − 138

13. 690
     − 481

14. 508
     − 137

15. 168
     − 39

16. 618
     − 476

17. 419
     − 59

18. 192
     − 108

19. 573
     − 468

20. 596
     − 128

21. 819
     − 124

22. 438
     − 283

Problem Solving

Think
What do I know?
What do I need to find?

DATA

Trip Distances

Trip	Miles
Cleveland to Chicago	346
Cincinnati to Cleveland	249
Washington, D.C., to Cleveland	372

23. How many more miles is it from Cleveland to Chicago than from Cincinnati to Cleveland?

24. Make Sense and Persevere Mr. Sousa is driving from Washington, D.C., to Cleveland and then to Cincinnati. He has traveled 182 miles. How many miles are left in his trip?

25. Make Sense and Persevere Which girl got more votes? How many more votes did that girl get?

DATA

Student Council President Votes

	7th Grade Votes	8th Grade Votes
Claudia	183	157
Jasmine	162	156

26. Kendra got $20 for her birthday. She earned $62 babysitting. Then she earned $148 shoveling snow. How much money does Kendra have?

$20	$62	$148

?

27. Higher Order Thinking Kim needs to find 437 − 258. Will she need to regroup to find the answer? If so, explain how she will need to regroup. What will Kim's answer be?

Assessment

28. It is 239 miles from Dallas to Houston and 275 miles from Dallas to San Antonio. How many fewer miles is it from Dallas to Houston than from Dallas to San Antonio?

Ⓐ 34 fewer miles
Ⓑ 36 fewer miles
Ⓒ 44 fewer miles
Ⓓ 45 fewer miles

29. An amusement park ride can hold 120 people. There are already 104 people on the ride. Which equation shows how many more people the ride can hold?

Ⓐ 120 − 104 = 16
Ⓑ 120 − 100 = 20
Ⓒ 120 − 94 = 26
Ⓓ 120 + 104 = 224

952

Lesson 9

Divide Regions into Equal Parts

I can... read and write a unit fraction.

I can also be precise in my work.

Solve

★
Solve & Share
★

Show two different ways to divide a 2 × 6 region into 6 equal parts. Color the 6 parts of each region a different color. How do you know the parts are equal?

Be precise. Think about each part as you divide the regions.

Look Back! **Use Structure** How are the parts of the regions alike? How are they different?

Digital Resources at SavvasRealize.com

How Can You Name the Equal Parts of a Whole?

A

Divide a whole into halves. What fraction can you write to represent one half of a whole?

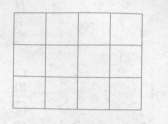

A fraction is an equal part of a whole.

B

one half

one half

Each part is made up of 6 unit squares. Both parts have equal areas.

C

$\frac{1}{2}$

$\frac{1}{2}$

Each part is **one** half of the area of the whole shape.

This fraction can be written as $\frac{1}{2}$.

$\frac{1}{2}$ is a unit fraction. A unit fraction represents one of the equal parts.

D

The number above the bar in a fraction is called the numerator.

The numerator shows the number of equal parts represented by that fraction.

numerator
denominator → → $\frac{1}{2}$

The number below the bar in a fraction is called the denominator.

The denominator shows the total number of equal parts in that whole.

Convince Me! **Be Precise** Divide the grid at the right into thirds. Label each third using a unit fraction. Explain how you knew which fraction to write.

Name

☆ Guided Practice

Do You Understand?

1. In the examples on page 954, explain how you know the two parts are equal.

In **2** and **3**, tell if each shows equal or unequal parts. If the parts are equal, label one of the parts using a unit fraction.

2.

3.

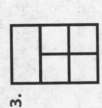

Do You Know How?

4. Draw a rectangle that is divided into fourths. Then, write the fraction that represents one equal part.

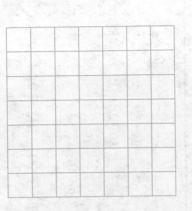

☆ Independent Practice ☆

In **5–7**, tell if each shows equal or unequal parts. If the parts are equal, name them.

5.

6.

7.

In **8** and **9**, draw lines to divide the shape into the given number of equal parts. Then write the fraction that represents one equal part.

8. 3 equal parts

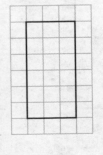

9. 8 equal parts

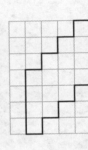

Problem Solving ☆

In 10-13, use the table of flags.

10. Which nation's flag is $\frac{1}{3}$ white?

11. Be Precise What fraction represents the red part of Poland's flag?

12. Which nation's flag does **NOT** have equal parts?

13. Which nation's flag is $\frac{1}{4}$ green?

Flags of Different Nations

Nation	Flag
Mauritius	
Nigeria	
Poland	
Seychelles	

14. Model with Math James buys 18 bottles of water. The water comes in packs of 6 bottles. How many packs did he buy? Write an addition equation and a multiplication equation to show your answer.

15. Higher Order Thinking Laura's books are shown below. What fraction of her books has a yellow cover?

< **Assessment**

16. On the grid below, draw a rectangle. Divide your rectangle into fourths. Explain how you checked the reasonableness of your work.

Lesson 10

Fractions and Regions

I can... show and name part of a region.

I can also make sense of problems.

Solve

Name _____

⭐ ☆
Solve & Share

Pat made a garden in the shape of a rectangle and divided it into 4 same-size parts. She planted flowers in one of the parts. Draw a picture of what Pat's garden might look like.

You can make sense of the given information to plan your drawing of Pat's garden.

Look Back! **Construct Arguments** How many parts of Pat's garden do **NOT** have flowers? Explain.

A-Z

How Can You Show and Name Part of a Region?

Essential Question

A

Mr. Peters served part of a pan of enchilada casserole to a friend. What does each part of the whole pan of casserole represent? What was served? What part is left?

A fraction is a symbol that names equal parts of a whole. A unit fraction represents one part of a whole that has been divided into equal parts. A unit fraction always has a numerator of 1.

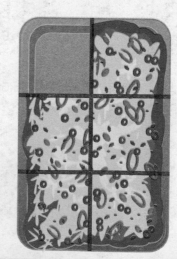

B What You Think

There are 6 equal pieces in the whole, so each piece is $\frac{1}{6}$.

There is 1 piece missing, so one $\frac{1}{6}$-piece was served.

There are 5 pieces left, so five $\frac{1}{6}$-pieces are left.

The numerator shows how many equal parts are described. The denominator shows the total number of equal parts in a whole.

C What You Write

$\frac{1}{6}$ ← numerator
← denominator

$\frac{1}{6}$ of the pan of enchilada casserole was served.

$\frac{5}{6}$ of the pan of enchilada casserole is left.

Do You Understand?

Convince Me! Model with Math Below is a picture of a pie pan. Draw lines and use shading to show that five $\frac{1}{8}$-pieces are still in the pan, and that three $\frac{1}{8}$-pieces were eaten. Remember to draw same-size parts.

958

☆ Guided Practice ☆

Do You Understand?

1. In the problem at the top of page 958, what fraction names all of the pieces in the casserole?

2. Model with Math Mrs. Rao made a cake. What fraction of the whole cake does each piece represent?

3. In the picture in Item 2, how many $\frac{1}{8}$-pieces were eaten? What fraction of the whole cake was eaten?

Do You Know How?

In **4** through **7**, use the figure below.

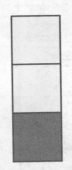

4. Write the unit fraction that represents each part of the whole.

5. How many $\frac{1}{3}$-parts are yellow?

6. What fraction of the whole is yellow?

7. What fraction names *all* of the parts in the whole?

☆ Independent Practice ☆

In **8** through **11**, write the unit fraction that represents each part of the whole. Then write the number of blue parts and the fraction of the whole that is blue.

8.

9.

10.

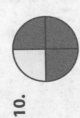

11.

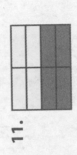

12. Draw a rectangle that shows 6 equal parts. Then shade $\frac{3}{6}$ of the rectangle. Explain how you know you shaded $\frac{3}{6}$ of the rectangle.

Problem Solving

13. Reasoning What is the distance around the baseball card? Write an equation to show and solve the problem.

6 cm

8 cm

---

14. Model with Math Janice has 2 scarves. Carla has 3 times as many scarves as Janice. How many scarves does Carla have? Use the bar diagram to write and solve an equation.

Janice → | 2 |

Carla → | 2 | 2 | 2 |

? scarves

15. Higher Order Thinking Draw a circle that shows 6 equal parts. Shade more than $\frac{3}{6}$ of the circle, but less than $\frac{5}{6}$ of the circle. What fraction have you modeled?

Assessment

In **16** and **17**, use the chart to the right.

16. Kiko and some friends bought a medium party tray. They ate 5 sections of the tray. Which of the following shows the unit fraction, and the fraction of the tray that was **NOT** eaten?

Ⓐ $\frac{1}{8}, \frac{3}{8}$

Ⓑ $\frac{1}{6}, \frac{4}{6}$

Ⓒ $\frac{8}{8}, \frac{2}{8}$

Ⓓ $\frac{1}{6}, \frac{1}{6}$

Size of Tray		Price
Small		$8
Medium		$10
Large		$12

In a unit fraction the numerator is always 1.

17. Jesse and his friends ordered a large party tray. Which unit fraction does each section of the tray represent?

Ⓐ $\frac{1}{4}$

Ⓑ $\frac{1}{6}$

Ⓒ $\frac{1}{8}$

Ⓓ $\frac{1}{10}$

960

Glossary

A

add

When you add, you join groups together.

$$3 + 4 = 7$$

addend

numbers that are added

$$2 + 5 = 7$$

↑ ↑

addends

after

424 comes after 423.

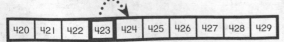

| 420 | 421 | 422 | 423 | 424 | 425 | 426 | 427 | 428 | 429 |

a.m.

clock time from midnight until noon

7:10 PM

angle

the corner shape formed by two sides that meet

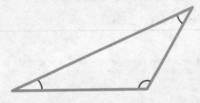

array

a group of objects set in equal rows and columns that forms a rectangle

B

bar diagram

a model for addition and subtraction that shows the parts and the whole

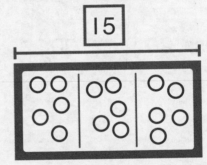

15

bar graph

A bar graph uses bars to show data.

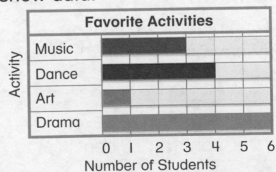

Favorite Activities

Activity: Music, Dance, Art, Drama

0 1 2 3 4 5 6

Number of Students

before

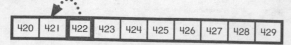

421 comes before 422.

---

break apart

You can break apart a number into its place value parts.

$$27 + 35 = ?$$

Tens: 20   30

Ones: 7   5

---

cents

The value of a coin is measured in cents (¢).

1 cent (¢)   10 cents (¢)

---

centimeter (cm)

a metric unit of length that is part of 1 meter

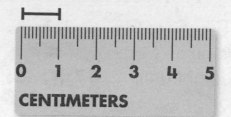

CENTIMETERS

---

coins

money that is made out of metal and that can have different values

1¢   5¢   10¢   25¢   50¢

---

column

objects in an array or data in a table that are shown up and down

← column

1	2	3	4	5
11	12	13	14	15
21	22	23	24	25
31	32	33	34	35

---

compare

When you compare numbers, you find out if a number is greater than, less than, or equal to another number.

$$147 \; > \; 143$$

147 is greater than 143.

---

compatible numbers

numbers that are easy to add or subtract using mental math

$$8 + 2$$
$$20 + 7$$
$$53 + 10$$

---

compensation

a mental math strategy you can use to add or subtract

$$38 + 24 = ?$$
$$+ 2 \quad - 2$$

You add 2 to 38 to make 40. Then subtract 2 from 24 to get 22. 40 + 22 = 62. So, 38 + 24 = 62.

cone

a solid figure with a circle shaped base and a curved surface that meets at a point

cube

a solid figure with six faces that are matching squares

cylinder

a solid figure with two matching circle shaped bases

 D

data

information you collect and can be shown in a table or graph

Favorite Fruit	
Apple	7
Peach	4
Orange	5

decrease

to become lesser in value

$$600 \longrightarrow 550$$

600 decreased by 50 is 550.

denominator

the number below the fraction bar in a fraction, which shows the total number of equal parts

$$\frac{3}{4} \longleftarrow \text{denominator}$$

difference

the answer in a subtraction equation or problem

$$14 - 6 = 8$$

$\uparrow$ difference

digits

 43

Numbers are made up of 1 or more digits. 43 has 2 digits.

dime

10 cents or 10¢

division

an operation that tells how many equal groups there are or how many are in each group

$$12 \div 3 = 4$$

divided by

what you say to read a division symbol

$$18 \div 3 = 6$$

↙ divided by

dollar

One dollar equals 100¢.

dollar bills

paper money that can have different dollar values, such as $1, $5, $10, or $20

dollar sign

a symbol used to show that a number represents money

$37

↑
dollar sign

doubles

addition facts that have two addends that are the same

$$4 + 4 = 8$$

↑ ↑
addend addend

E

edge

a line formed where two faces of a solid figure meet

edge

eighths

When a whole is separated into 8 equal shares, the parts are called eighths.

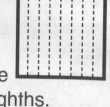

equal groups

groups that have the same number of items or objects

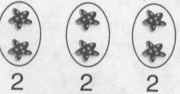

2   2   2

equal shares

parts of a whole that are the same size

All 4 shares are equal.

equals (=)

has the same value

$$36 = 36$$

36 is equal to 36.

equation

a math sentence that uses an equal sign (=) to show that the value on the left is equal to the value on the right

$$3 + ? = 7$$

$$14 - 6 = 8$$

estimate

When you estimate, you make a good guess.

This table is about 3 feet long.

even

a number that can be shown as a pair of cubes.

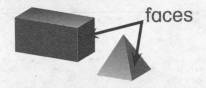

8 is even.

expanded form

a way of writing a number that shows the place value of each digit

$$400 + 60 + 3 = 463$$

face

a flat surface of a solid figure that does not roll

faces

fact family

a group of related addition and subtraction facts

$$2 + 4 = 6$$

$$4 + 2 = 6$$

$$6 - 2 = 4$$

$$6 - 4 = 2$$

factors

numbers that are multiplied together to give a product

$$7 \times 3 = 21$$

factors

flat surface

flat surfaces that are **NOT** faces

foot (ft)

a standard unit of length equal to 12 inches

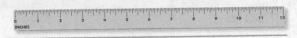

fourths

When a whole is divided into 4 equal shares, the shares are called fourths.

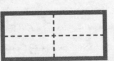

fraction

a number, such as $\frac{1}{2}$ or $\frac{3}{4}$, that names part of a whole or part of a set

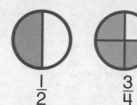

$\frac{1}{2}$ $\frac{3}{4}$

 G

greater than (>)

has greater value

5 > 1

5 is greater than 1.

---

greatest

the number in a group with the largest value

35 47 58 61
greatest

greatest value

The coin that has the greatest value is the coin that is worth the most.

The quarter has the greatest value.

H

half-dollar

50 cents or 50¢

---

half past

30 minutes past the hour

It is half past 9.

halves (half)

When a whole is divided into 2 equal shares, the shares are called halves.

---

height

how tall an object is from bottom to top

---

heptagon

a polygon that has 7 sides

---

hexagon

a polygon that has 6 sides

---

hour

An hour is 60 minutes.

---

hundred

10 tens make 1 hundred.

inch (in.)

a standard unit of length that is part of 1 foot

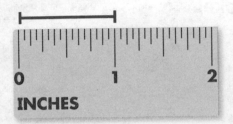

increase

to become greater in value

$$550 \longrightarrow 600$$

550 increased by 50 is 600.

least

the number in a group with the smallest value

35 47 58 61
↳ least

least value

The coin that has the least value is the coin that is worth the least.

The dime has the least value.

length

the distance from one end to the other end of an object

less than (<)

has less value

$$2 < 6$$

2 is less than 6.

line plot

A line plot uses dots above a number line to show data.

Lengths of Shells

Number of Inches

M

Start at 23. Count on 2 tens. 33, 43

mental math

math you do in your head

$$23 + 20 = 43$$

meter (m)

a metric unit of length equal to 100 centimeters

A long step is about a meter.

minute

a standard length of time
There are 60 minutes in 1 hour.

multiplication

an operation that gives the total number when you join equal groups

$$3 \times 2 = 6$$

To multiply 3×2 means to add 2 three times.

$$2 + 2 + 2 = 6$$

near doubles

addition facts that have two addends that are close

$$4 + 5 = 9$$

↑   ↑
addend addend

nearest centimeter

The whole number centimeter mark closest to the measure is the nearest centimeter.

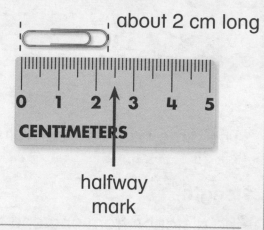

about 2 cm long

CENTIMETERS

halfway mark

nearest inch

The whole number inch mark closest to the measure is the nearest inch.

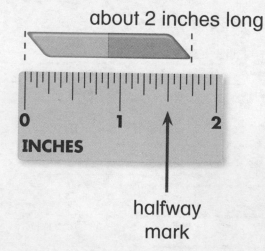

about 2 inches long

INCHES

halfway mark

next ten

the first ten greater than a number

30 is the next ten after 27.

nickel

5 cents or 5¢

nonagon

a polygon that has 9 sides

number line

a line that shows numbers in order from left to right

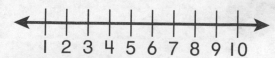

1 2 3 4 5 6 7 8 9 10

numerator

the number above the fraction bar in a fraction, which shows how many equal parts are described

$\frac{3}{4}$ ←——— numerator

octagon

a polygon that has 8 sides

odd

a number that can **NOT** be shown as pairs of cubes

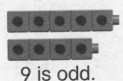

9 is odd.

ones

digits that shows how many ones are in a number

$$54 + 14 = 68$$

open number line

An open number line is a tool that can help you add or subtract. It can begin at any number.

$$26 + 20 = 46$$

order

to place numbers from least to greatest or from greatest to least

27 72 107 117 171

least   greatest

P

parallelogram

a quadrilateral that has 4 sides and opposite sides parallel

part

a piece of a whole or of a number

2 and 3 are parts of 5.

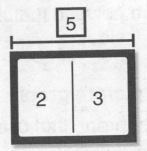

partial sum

When you add numbers, the sum of one of the place values is called a partial sum.

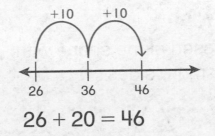

Tens	Ones	
5	7	
+ 2	8	
7	0	← partial sum
+ 1	5	← partial sum
8	5	← sum

penny

1 cent or 1¢

pentagon

a polygon that has 5 sides

picture graph

a graph that uses pictures to show data

Favorite Ball Games	
Baseball	
Soccer	
Tennis	

Each = I student

place-value chart

a chart matches each digit of a number with its place

Hundreds	Tens	Ones
3	4	8

plane shape

a flat shape

  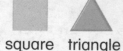

circle   rectangle   square   triangle

p.m.

clock time from noon until midnight

polygon

a closed plane shape with 3 or more sides

product

the answer to a multiplication problem

$$4 \times 2 = 8$$

↑
product

pyramid

a solid figure with a base that is a polygon and faces that are triangles that meet in a point

Q

quadrilateral

a polygon that has 4 sides

quarter

25 cents or 25¢

quarter past

15 minutes after the hour

It is quarter past 4.

quarter to

15 minutes before the hour

It is quarter to 4.

G10

Glossary

R

rectangular prism

a solid figure with bases and faces that are rectangles

regroup

to name a number or part in a different way

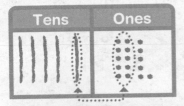

10 ones can be regrouped as 1 ten. 1 ten can be regrouped as 10 ones.

related

Addition facts and subtraction facts are related if they have the same numbers.

$$2 + 3 = 5$$
$$5 - 2 = 3$$

repeated addition

adding the same number repeatedly

$$3 + 3 + 3 + 3 = 12$$

right angle

an angle that forms a square corner

row

objects in an array or data in a table that are shown across

1	2	3	4	5
11	12	13	14	15
21	22	23	24	25
31	32	33	34	35

← row

S

separate

to subtract or to take apart into two or more parts

$$5 - 2 = 3$$

side

a line segment that makes one part of a plane shape

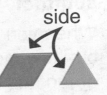
side

solid figure

a shape that has length, width, and height

These are all solid figures.

sphere

a solid figure that looks like a ball

standard form

a way to write a number using only digits

436

subtract

When you subtract, you find out how many are left or which group has more.

$$5 - 3 = 2$$

sum

the answer to an addition equation or problem

$$3 + 4 = 7$$

$$\begin{array}{r} 4 \\ +3 \\ \hline 7 \end{array}$$

sum $\longrightarrow$ 7

symbol

a picture or character that stands for something

The symbol will be 🧍.
Each 🧍 represents
1 student.

T

tally mark

a symbol used to keep track of each piece of information in an organized list

Ways to Show 30¢

Quarter	Dime	Nickel	Total
I		I	30¢
	III		30¢
	II	II	30¢
	I	IIII	30¢
		IIII I	30¢

tens

the digit that shows how many groups of ten are in a number

238
↑

thirds

When a whole is divided into 3 equal shares, the shares are called thirds.

thousand

10 hundreds make 1 thousand.

times

another word for multiply

times

$$7 \times 3 = 21$$

trapezoid

a polygon with 4 sides and one pair of sides are parallel

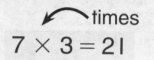

triangular prism

a solid figure that has two triangle shaped bases and three faces that have rectangle shapes.

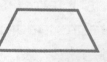

U

unequal

Unequal parts are parts that are not equal.

5 unequal parts

unit

You can use different units to measure.

about 12 inches
about 1 foot

unit fraction

a fraction that reperesents one equal part of a whole or a set

$\frac{1}{2}$ $\frac{1}{4}$ $\frac{1}{8}$

unknown

a symbol that stands for a number in an equation

$$34 + ? = 67$$

↑
unknown

V

vertices (vertex)

corner points where 2 sides of a polygon meet or where edges of a solid figure meet

vertex

W

whole

a single unit that can be divided into parts

The two halves make one whole circle.

width

the distance across an object

word form

a way to write a number using only words

The word form for 23 is twenty-three.

Y

yard (yd)

a standard unit of length equal to 3 feet

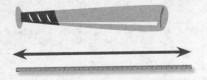

A baseball bat is about a yard long.

Photographs

Photo locators denoted as follows: Top (T), Center (C), Bottom (B), Left (L), Right (R), Background (Bkgd)

001BL Lori Martin/Shutterstock;**001BR** An Nguyen/Shutterstock;**001C** Africa Studio/Fotolia;**001L** Africa Studio/Fotolia;**001R** karandaev/Fotolia;**077BL** michaklootwijk/Fotolia;**077BR** Jitka Volfova/Shutterstock;**077L** Charles Brutlag/Shutterstock;**077R** Erni/Fotolia;**119L** FiCo74/Fotolia;**119R** Antonio Scarpi/Fotolia;**189** Beboy/Shutterstock;**253** Deborah Benbrook/Fotolia;**321** GlebStock/Shutterstock;**389** Paylessimages/Fotolia;**435** Ambient Ideas/Shutterstock;**503** Es0lex/Fotolia;**583** kalafoto/Fotolia;**635** Klagyivik Viktor/Shutterstock;**675** Nagel Photography/Shutterstock;**678** Optionm/Shutterstock;**687** Ant Clausen/Fotolia;**759** Bonita R. Cheshier/Shutterstock;**788** Lledó/Fotolia;**790** Ivan Kruk/Fotolia;**799L** Karichs/Fotolia;**799R** Ivonne Wierink/Fotolia;**851** Yurakr/Shutterstock;**868** StudioSmart/Shutterstock;**G10R** United State Mint.

Neighborhood Song

Trish Holland

TeachingStrategies® · Bethesda, MD

For Teaching Strategies, LLC.
Publisher: Larry Bram
Editorial Director: Hilary Parrish Nelson
VP Curriculum and Assessment: Cate Heroman
Product Manager: Kai-leé Berke
Book Development Team: Sherrie Rudick and Jan Greenberg
Project Manager: Jo A. Wilson

For Q2AMedia
Editorial Director: Bonnie Dobkin
Editor and Curriculum Adviser: Suzanne Barchers
Program Manager: Gayatri Singh
Creative Director: Simmi Sikka
Project Manager: Santosh Vasudevan
Designer: Ritu Chopra
Picture Researchers: Judy Brown & Stephanie Mills

Picture Credits
t-top b-bottom c-center l-left r-right

Cover: Jurgen Magg/Jupiter.

Back Cover: Keith Brofsky/Photolibrary.

Title page: Jurgen Magg/Jupiter.

Insides: Frances M Roberts/Photolibrary: 3, Keith Brofsky/Photolibrary: 4, Keith Levit Photography/Photolibrary: 5, Morgan Lane Photography/Shutterstock: 6, Masterfile: 7, Jupiter Images: 8, Mike Brake/Shutterstock: 9, Vadim Kozlovsky/Dreamstime: 10, Stephen Coburn/Dreamstime: 11l, Stephen Coburn/Dreamstime: 11r, Monkey Business Images Ltd./Photolibrary: 12, SW Productions/Photolibrary: 13t, Monkey Business Images Ltd./Photolibrary: 13b, Alex Mares-Manton/Photolibrary: 14, Stephen Coburn/Pam Ostrow/Jupiter Images: 15t, Avava/Dreamstime: 15b, Peter Bennett/Photolibrary: 16, Corbis/Jupiter Images: 17, Lisa F.Young/Shutterstock: 18, Mark Hunt/Photolibrary: 19, Jurgen Magg/Jupiter Images: 20, Ariell Skelley/Jupiter Images: 21, Rmarmion/Dreamstime: 22, Istockphoto: 23t, Robert Dowey/Photolibrary: 23b, Ryan McVay/Photolibrary: 24.

Teaching Strategies, LLC.
Bethesda, MD
www.TeachingStrategies.com

ISBN: 978-1-60617-143-1

Library of Congress Cataloging-in-Publication Data
Holland, Trish.
  Neighborhood song / Trish Holland.
      p. cm.
  ISBN 978-1-60617-143-1
  1. Neighborhoods--Juvenile literature. 2. Neighbors--Juvenile literature. I. Title.
  HM761.H65 2010
  307--dc22
                                    2009044287
CPSIA tracking label information:
RR Donnelley, Shenzhen, China
Date of Production: Nov 2016
Cohort: Batch 6

Printed and bound in China

8 9 10	17 16
Printing	Year Printed

This is the way we live together,
Live together, live together.
This is the way we live together
In our neighborhood.

This is the way we travel around,
Travel around, travel around.
This is the way we travel around
In our neighborhood.

This is the way we go to school,
Go to school, go to school.
This is the way we go to school
In our neighborhood.

These are the people who care for us,
Care for us, care for us.
These are the people who care for us
In our neighborhood.

This is the way we do our work,
Do our work, do our work.
This is the way we do our work
In our neighborhood.

This is the way we get our food,
Get our food, get our food.
This is the way we get our food
In our neighborhood.

This is the way we get our clothes,
Get our clothes, get our clothes.
This is the way we get our clothes
In our neighborhood.

This is the way we keep things nice,
Keep things nice, keep things nice.
This is the way we keep things nice
In our neighborhood.

This is the way we help our neighbors,
Help our neighbors, help our neighbors.
This is the way we help our neighbors
In our neighborhood.

This is the way we play together,
Play together, play together.
This is the way we play together
In our neighborhood.

This is the way we get together,
Get together, get together.
This is the way we get together
In our neighborhood.

This is the way we celebrate,
Celebrate, celebrate.
This is the way we celebrate
In our neighborhood.